The Effects of the Factory System

BY

ALLEN CLARKE

WRITTEN 1895-6
REVISED 1897-8

LONDON
GRANT RICHARDS
9 HENRIETTA STREET, COVENT GARDEN, W.C.
1899

First published 1899.
This edition 1985.

ISBN 0 946571 05 8 *hardback*
ISBN 0,946571 06 6 *paperback*

Published by
George Kelsall Publishing
The Bookshop, 22 Church Street,
Littleborough, Lancashire, OL15 9AA
tel 0706 70244

Printed & Bound by
Smith Settle
Otley, West Yorkshire

ACKNOWLEDGEMENTS

Mrs Dorothy Dewhurst, Allen Clarke's daughter, ·
for her kind permission to republish her father's writings.

Bolton Public Libraries including
Farnworth Branch Library.

Bolton Museums and Art Gallery.

Oldham Local Studies Library.

Mrs Olive, Bolton.

Anne Catterson, Bolton.

THE EFFECTS OF THE FACTORY SYSTEM
by Allen Clarke.

Written in 1895-6, partly serialised in *The Clarion*.
First published in book form by Grant Richards,
London, 1899.

Introduction by Paul Salveson

Allen Clarke's *Effects of the Factory System* is a forgotten classic of British social criticism. It was written fifty years after Engels' *Condition of the Working Class* at a time when the Lancashire cotton industry had world wide supremacy. However, this is not the work of an outsider, however well-intentioned. Clarke had first hand experience of 'the factory system' as a child, and both his parents were cotton workers. Neither is it the dull recital of facts and figures alone; though Clarke wanted to produce a factual criticism of the evils of factory life in the book his bitterness towards the system still shouts from each page. It is a truly revolutionary book which made Clarke few friends, and many enemies. The hard-nosed Lancashire mill-owners get their just desserts, but so do the complacent union officials, career politicians and easily-impressed sociologists. The cotton workers themselves don't emerge as heroic figures — they are ground down by the system, mentally and physically. Rather than fight the system, they are prepared to accept palliatives within it — a few pence on their wages, a few minutes off the working day. Their children are sent out to work half-time in the mills, risking death or injury, for a couple of extra shillings a week. Indeed, so harsh is his criticism of the factory workers themselves that it is remarkable how he retained the love and admiration of countless thousands of them — who eagerly read his dialect sketches and popular journalism. Indeed, in his chapter on "The Future" he tries to reassure himself:

. . . surely these folks will never hate me — one of themselves, a factory lad, son of factory father and mother, brother to brothers and sisters in the factory today, a faithful comrade and their best well-wisher — for showing the truth, and praying for their salvation. (page 173)

Today the mule spinners and power loom weavers are gone. Like the handloom weavers who preceded them, they are an extinct race. The Lancashire cotton industry is now all but dead — its end being prophesied by this book back in 1896. Lancashire people today are spared the evils that Clarke describes though I doubt whether he would be very impressed by what we have in its place. The drudgery of the mill is gone, but so too is the comradeship and warmth that made it just about bearable.

This short book was originally written to draw the nation's attention to the reality of life in the Lancashire cotton industry; to show the immense evil which lay beneath the immense riches of the British Empire, and, tentatively, confusingly, to suggest a better way. Today the book deserves to be read as a reminder of those days by the grandsons and grand-daughters of those weavers and spinners. It should be read by children in school (and it isn't a difficult book to read) to show them that if they had been alive in the Bolton of the 1890s, they too would be rising at 5 and trudging to their work with all the deafening noise, bullying, injury, exhaustion and often death that faced the children of those days.

This is the real heritage of the Lancashire people — a dark heritage too. There is also a bright and honourable side to it, in the people like Allen Clarke who both fought the system and attempted to make life a bit brighter for the victims of it.

Allen Clarke

Clarke was born in Bolton, in 1863 – at the height of the Cotton Famine. His father was a spinner and active trade unionist. His mother was a winder in the mill. He himself began work at the age of 11 as a little piecer — the dangerous work of assisting the mule spinner 'piece-up' the broken threads being spun on the gigantic mule. He then did various jobs as an errand boy before going back to the mill, at Cross's of Gilnow. The owner, Joseph Cross, encouraged the young piecer and Clarke left the following year to become a pupil teacher at Hulton Street School. He began writing seriously and won many competitions; he finally tired of teaching, wanting to make journalism his career. He got an office job with the *Bolton Evening News*, hoping it would be a stepping stone into the world of journalism. At the same time, in the late 1880s, Clarke became politically involved, joining the Marxist-based Social Democratic Federation at the time of the big Engineers' Strike of 1887. After numerous disappointments he left the *Evening News* and took the somewhat rash step of setting up what he claimed was Lancashire's first labour newspaper — *The Labour Light* — without a halfpenny of capital. Fortunately his printers gave him credit and the paper paid its way for a short while. It was a combination of union reports, news and some very funny dialect sketches. This was where *Bill and Bet Spriggs* first saw the light of day — based on a suggestion by the printer to make *The Labour Light* a bit lighter to read! Though the paper folded within a year, he went on to edit *The Bolton Trotter* from 1891. This was a popular, satirical local magazine with a socialist slant. It sold exceedingly well though he was often threatened with libel actions. Clarke's journalistic career was now well and truly launched and he went on to work for the *Cotton Factory Times* and then to edit his own *Teddy Ashton's Northern Weekly* from 1896 to 1908. In his *Tum Fowt* dialect sketches Clarke used the pseudonym of "Teddy Ashton", by which name he became far more famous than "Allen Clarke".

His writing output was immense. As well as writing for the above papers, he was also a frequent writer for a host of local and labour-inclined papers such as *Rochdale Labour News*, *The Labour Leader*, *Clarion* and others including the spiritualist paper *The Two Worlds*. His dialect sketches were sold as penny pamphlets and sales eventually totalled over a million. He wrote a considerable amount of poetry — both in dialect and in standard English. His first collection, *Voices*, was published by *The Clarion* in 1896 and contained a hard-hitting poem called "Voice of the Half-Timers", which ends like this:

> If Christ coom lookin' Lancashire though,
> An' seed us hauve-timers at wark an' skoo,
> What would he say neaw? — What would He do?
> Us plagued mites know! An' yo' done too!
> Why he'd punce an' pummel yo' black an' blue!
> An' then, maybe, for a change o' show,
> Make parents of us an' childer o' yo,

(If He thowt fit he could yessy do that
For he were a dab wi't conjurin' hat).
So yo' could larn what it's like for t'be
Hauve-time in skoo an' factory,
An' then — but we couldn't make things wuss,
For we couldn't treat yo' as yo' treat us!

Earlier, Clarke had been involved with J. R. Clynes, the future Cabinet Minister but then a little piecer from Oldham, in an attempt to form a Piecer's Union. It incurred the wrath of employer, spinner, and spinner's unions and quickly died. His work for the piecers' agitation is reflected in *Effects of the Factory System*, which contains a large section on children's conditions.

In between all this, he managed to write over twenty novels of working class life. Most of them were serialised in the *Cotton Factory Times* and *Northern Weekly* and only a minority ever appeared in book form. The first to do so was *The Lass At The Man And Scythe* about the Civil War in Bolton in the 1640s. Most of his later novels had a contemporary setting. *The Knobstick* was set at the time of the Great Engineers' Strike of 1887, and *Lancashire Lasses And Lads* is about modern life in the mills. In many ways, the novel is a literary version of *Effects of the Factory System*. Take this excerpt, where Harold Bennett and Dick Dickinson are walking into Bolton (Spindleton) early in the morning:

Spindleton — at any rate, the poorer working portion of it — was now waking up. Almost all at once the upper bedroom window of cottage after cottage started into yellow light.

Harold had been silent the last twenty minutes of the walk.

Dick spoke. "The town's getting up to its work," he said, "though I'm afraid most of the older folks are grumbling at

*having to rise, and the younger ones are being dragged out of
bed. Hark the hideous steam buzzers are beginning to shriek.
The knocker-ups are busy rattling at the windows; the toilers
surlily jump up and tap back at the pane, growling, 'What —
time to get up already? I'm sure I've nobbut just come to bed.
Eh, I could do wi' just another turn o'er.' They are spluttering
about in the dark, shivering as they stick their legs into icy
trousers and skirts, and wishing the factories were at the bottom
of the sea. In a few minutes the streets will be full of the great
glum procession hurrying to the mills and workshops."*
(*Lancashire Lasses and Lads* page 9)

It is fashionable amongst some historians today to
claim that life in the mills was just like being part of one
big, happy family, with seaside trips organised by the
masters and birthday parties for the masters' sons and
daughters. Allen Clarke's writing — and the testimony
of many who are still alive to remember those days —
gives another side to the story.

Clarke badly wanted an alternative to the life he
describes in his novels and in this book. He joined all
sorts of political groupings — the Social Democratic
federation, the Independent Labour Party, the Labour
Church and was interested in anarchist ideas. He stood
as socialist candidate in the 1900 General Election in
Rochdale and four years later was closely involved in an
attempt to build a socialist commune at Daisy Colony,
near Blackpool. This, he hoped, would become a haven
for the oppressed factory worker and the example would
spread throughout Lancashire and to the rest of the
country. Indeed, this image of a de-industrialised Lancashire of small scale production first emerges in this book:

*I would like to see Lancashire a cluster of small villages and
towns, each fixed solid on its own agricultural base, doing its*

> *own spinning and weaving, with its theatre, gymnasium, schools, libraries, baths and all things necessary for body and soul.* (page 174)

These hopes — and those of the whole socialist movement — were shattered by the catastrophe of the Great War. At the end of it, the bright socialist vision that had inspired thousands years before was dead. In its place was a dogmatic communism inspired by the Russian Revolution, and a placid, bureaucratic reformism of the Labour Party. Clarke had no place in either arrangement. He continued to write his dialect sketches, publish his *Lancashire Annual* each Christmas, and write mainly for the *Liverpool Weekly Post*. In 1926 he gave considerable support in his writings to the miners on strike. He died at Blackpool in 1935, as he was just about to take up flying as a hobby. He was probably one of the best loved men of Lancashire, and still remembered today as "Teddy Ashton".

The Effects of the Factory System

The core of the book was originally serialised in Robert Blatchford's socialist weekly paper *The Clarion* in 1895-6. It was revised the following year and published, as a longer work, by Grant Richards in 1899. In an editorial in *The Northern Weekly* of 26th March 1904, he describes the work that went into writing the book: going through mounds of statistics, reports, articles. Let him speak for himself:

> *Why did I write this book? Because it seemed to me necessary, for the cause of progress, that such a book should be written. Many books and pamphlets dealing with the history of the factory system, and the struggles of factory workers to obtain better conditions of labour, had been written but so far nobody*

> *had ever made a systematic investigation of the factory system and its effects on the people. Now I thought I had certain qualifications for this task. I had lived all my life amongst factory folks. I had worked in a cotton mill myself. I had for years taught in a day school in a factory town, thus coming into very close contact with factory children and their home life, and I had also worked, and was still working, on a paper which is in a sense the organ of the factory operatives — 'The Cotton Factory Times'. I had thus had ample opportunity of studying factory life, both from the inside and the outside; both in its effects on adults and on children; and I thought I would do my best to write as fair and impartial a criticism as I could on the subject.*

Initially, the book did not make much of a stir. However, it must have sold well enough, for the publishers brought out a paper edition in 1904. *The Daily Mail* got hold of a copy and ran a piece on it headed "A Terrible Book — The Tragedy of Lancashire"! It was said that 'all England should read it' but also that some parts of it could not be true. Furthermore, it was neither literary nor eloquent! The review got the book into the public eye at least. Controversy raged with Clarke being accused by "Mancunian" in *The Daily Mail* of 'ridiculous flights of hysterical rhetoric'. The issue was joined by *The Textile Mercury* — the journal of the most reactionary cotton employers. Clarke, it said, had libelled Lancashire! A further letter in the same journal by a "T. Owen" accuses him of deliberately falsifying facts and figures. Clarke replied:

> *Perhaps T. Owen would say that the working classes have no right to the same health and leisure as the moneyed classes. But I say — and can prove it if need be, that the workers have more right to health and happiness than capitalists, bankers,*

financiers, solicitors, army and navy officers, merchants, traders, writers, journalists and even statesmen. For the working classes keep all of these; and — I say this carefully — the most depraved of the workers is really a better man than the best of the idlers who live on his labour. (in *Teddy Ashton's Northern Weekly* 2nd April 1904)

The importance of Clarke's book was recognised in some surprising circles — Leo Tolstoy the great Russian libertarian thinker had the book translated and wrote to Clarke congratulating him on his works. Indeed, the solutions offered by Clarke at the end of the book clearly owe much to Tolstoy's ideas of self-governing communes working the land and engaging in small scale industry. Presumably the book was less well received in the orthodox circles of British social-democracy. Utopianism, neglect of the doctrine of class warfare, romanticism etc would, I'm sure, be some of the criticisms slung at the book, both then and today. Yet some of Clarke's utopian vision is needed today if socialism is to become once again a popular and inspiring force; and what he is saying isn't that different from what a lot of environmentalists in 'the green lobby' are saying throughout the world. The factory system of Clarke's day is gone — what do we put in its place? Robots or human beings?

Bolton Then and Now

It's worth commenting briefly on the Bolton of Clarke's day, and Bolton now. He mentions the 152 cotton spinning firms (not mills — there were often three or four to each firm). Today, I know of about half a dozen mills still working in this area. Bolton's engineering industry — at its height in the 1890s with Hicks, Dobson and Barlow and other great names — is now reduced to a handful of small scale factories under an ever-present threat of closure. Many of the mills have been demolished, some remain as scruffy, under-utilised 'units' employing twos and threes in cheap car repair businesses. Unemployment is at 16% — the worst it's ever been, even in the 1930s.

When Allen Clarke was writing his book Lancashire, and Bolton as a big part of it, genuinely was 'the workshop of the world'. Now the old productive base of Lancashire and the north based on cotton, coal and steel has been destroyed leaving little in its place. The people of Lancashire are much the same, though the cultural complexion has become more varied with immigration from India and Pakistan in the 1960s. Allen Clarke was the son of an Irish immigrant who left his native country for many of the same reasons that the Asian people left their homes: poverty, repression and the hope for a better life. Lancashire people are basically tolerant and good-hearted and if many of Clarke's criticisms of them remain today, we should blame the system they live under. A last word from him:

> *The factory system is bad. But the factory folk are a deal better than the system. Not in health and body, but in grit and good-humour; and they would be a fine set of people if they had only a chance to develop themselves under fair conditions.* (in *Teddy Ashton's Northern Weekly* 2.4.1904)

Postscript

Allen Clarke wrote a vast amount of books, sketches, pamphlets. Most of these are long since out of print, but all Lancashire libraries will have some of his works, usually as reference copies. If you want to get to know the work of Clarke better, read a few of his *Tum Fowt* sketches (written as "Teddy Ashton"). Two good novels to start with are *The Knobstick* and *Lancashire Lasses and Lads*. *Moorlands and Memories* is a marvellous book about Lancashire's moors, *Windmill Land* is about the characters and scenery of Fylde's 'windmill land'. If your library doesn't have the copy you want, order through inter-library loans.

Paul Salveson

ILLUSTRATIONS

CONTENTS

CONTENTS

THE EFFECTS OF THE FACTORY SYSTEM

SECTION I

INTRODUCTORY

CHAPTER I

THE MODERN FACTORY SYSTEM AND CONTEMPORARY EVENTS

THE nineteenth century is the machine age, with the god of steam (now aided, and to some extent superseded, by electricity) in the machine. Since James Watt, in 1764, discovered how to utilise the power of steam, men have decreased in marketable price, while machinery has increased in value. To-day men are of less consequence than machines: they are the servants of machines. The machine, in its wonderful development, has become almost human; while man has been reduced, as far as possible, to the condition of a machine. The modern worker is at the mercy of machinery. It is his pitiless master; it robs him of his wages; it pushes his fellows out of employment; it

A

regulates his hours of toil, his food-time, his
play-time. The workers of to-day are like a number of mechanical figures set in motion by, and
revolving round, a huge steam-engine. One does
not wonder that in the early days, when iron
first was brought into competition with flesh
and blood, the workers rose in wrath and tried
to destroy all the new machinery. Probably
they foresaw the usurpation and slavery that
were coming. Not that the machinery in itself
was, or is, such a bad thing; its curse lay in
its being the property of the capitalists, who
soon realised what vast fortunes they could cap-
ture by its use. Iron, ingeniously fashioned into
a giant's body, with a venous system of steam,
leathern muscles called straps, and Mammon for
soul or guiding power, became a monster that
snatched hand-workers from their homes, dragged
them to one of his dungeons, and said, "Here
shall you be my slaves, or starve."

And so, though agriculture was improved by
better drainage, manuring, and application of
chemistry, and from 1760 to 1834 nearly seven
million acres of waste land were reclaimed, yet
"England was transformed from a grain-exporting
to a grain-importing country,"[1] because the capitalists saw that fortunes were to be made more
quickly in manufacture than in agriculture; and
then, as all attention was devoted to manufacture,

[1] "Condition of Working-Classes in England in 1844,"
by Engels, p. 13.

the improvements in agriculture did not keep pace with the inventions and improvements in manufacture, but soon fell far behind. England gave up its corn for iron; because the iron made gold for the few.

The people flocked to the towns; were forced there to get work. Values of land went up. The iron demon made money for everybody except the workers. The big fortunes of England, especially those of the capitalist class, have been acquired this century. The iron demon has done well, seemingly, for those who caught and compelled him to their service. I say "seemingly," because in the end he will turn on his masters, as the fiend always does in the old soul-selling legends, and they will find they have been terribly taken in. For though the iron demon has made luxury for the few, he has made poverty and crime and feelings of rebellion for the many; and out of these two things—fat tyranny on the one hand and lean slavery on the other—no good can come, but only evil.

Indeed, the retribution began soon and strangely. Most of the inventors of the machines that were to change Lancashire (and England) so much, died poor and desolate. The curse of poverty, in an ironical fate and ill-omened foreboding, fell first on those who invented the machines that should place the many in the power of the few.

Samuel Crompton (inventor of the spinning-mule) died penniless; and I have been told that one of his male relatives was fetched out of Bolton Workhouse to walk in the procession when the inventor's statue was unveiled in Bolton in 1863; and was, as soon as the ceremony to the inventor's honour was over, hurried back to his workhouse fare, while those who had made fortunes out of the spinning-mule went to feast gloriously. What a fine picture this incident would make: the pauper from the workhouse humbly standing in the applauding crowd, while the men of money paid their debts to his dead brother, whom in life they had neglected, by uncovering a bronze statue to his memory.[1] John Kay of Bury, inventor of the fly-shuttle, died in obscurity in a foreign land. James Hargreaves of Standhill, Blackburn, inventor of the spinning-jenny, was also driven from his native country.[2]

[1] Samuel Crompton was a noble, unselfish fellow. He *gave* his invention to his country : trusting to his countrymen's honour and justice to be paid fairly for it. Honour and justice, however, are evidently no part of the commercial spirit : Crompton got little or nothing from those to whom he gave all. His biographer, French, says of him, "Had he studied human nature with one tithe of the skill and energy he devoted to his mechanical pursuits, his name would have ranked now among the highest in the nation, and his posterity among the wealthiest of its commercial aristocracy." That is to say, had he been more of a knave and less of an honest man, he would have "got on." Samuel Crompton's glory is that he died poor ; and his glory is the shame of his generation. I revere Crompton because he did not become one of "the wealthiest of the commercial aristocracy,"—like Arkwright.

[2] French's "Life of Samuel Crompton," p. 14.

These inventions were quickly followed by others, all working to one object—the beginning of the modern factory system. In 1785, six years after Crompton had finished his spinning-mule, Watt's steam-engine was first used for motive power. Fourteen years prior to this date, and four years after his invention, or appropriation, of the spinning-throstle in 1767 (the year when canals were first cut on an extensive scale), Arkwright had built his first factory at Cromford, in Derbyshire; and though this was the real beginning of the modern factory system, the motive power was water in its common liquid state, and not as steam.

In 1786 the biggest spinning - mule in Bolton had only 108 spindles; to - day there are mules containing 1200 spindles. This contrast shows the great mechanical progress of the last hundred years.

A brief summary of the successive steps in the development of the factory system tabulated side by side with contemporaneous movements, thought, progress, and literature, makes a very instructive and interesting piece of industrial and human history.

In 1730 the use of the word " factory " occurs for the first time in a Bolton rate-book. In 1738, Kay of Bury invents the fly-shuttle; and John Wesley is beginning the great Methodist movement. About 1740, weaver and merchant, who had hitherto been equal in social status, begin to diverge socially, the merchant going up as the weaver goes down. In 1760, the year of the conquest of Canada, there were only 40,000 persons employed in the cotton trade in the British Isles; to-day (1897) there are over half-a-million. The rapid development of the cotton trade began with the invention of the steam-engine,[1] followed by the invention of Hargreaves' spinning-jenny (1764),[2] and Arkwright's spinning-throstle (1767). In 1771, a year after Gold-smith published "The Deserted Village," and Huntsman first made steel ingots at Attercliffe (1770), Arkwright opened his first factory at Cromford (it was run by water-power). And in this year, which practically began the modern factory system, was born Robert Owen, who became an opponent of the factory system, and eventually set up a Socialist community in Indiana, U.S.A.

The age of machinery was now fairly started, and mechanical inventions quickly followed each other. It is also singular to note that Wesleyan Methodism spread rapidly at this time; machinery and Methodism grew up together in the North. Also with the factory system began modern Poli-tical Economy; in 1776 Adam Smith published his "Wealth of Nations."

[1] The invention of the steam-engine is dated 1764 by Engels, 1769 by Gibbins.

[2] The invention of the spinning-jenny is dated 1764 by Engels, 1767 by French, 1770 by Gibbins.

In 1779, five years after America assumed independence, Samuel Crompton of Hall-i'-th'-Wood, Bolton, invented the spinning-mule, of which John Bright said, "Without this machine we should all relapse into barbarism," and at this time machine-breaking riots began. A year later (1780) Robert Raikes started Sunday schools; in 1781, England, after long war, totally lost her American colonies; in 1783 Montgolfier sent up the first balloon (at Versailles); in 1784 George Stephenson built his first locomotive; in 1785, soon after the poet Crabbe had written his poems on village life to tell the rich the sufferings of the poor, the first steam-engine was used as motive power, and Burns was writing his poems of love of lass, love of man, and love of nature; in 1786 died Tim Bobbin, the first Lancashire dialect writer; in 1787 the Argand lamp was invented while in 1788, Tom Paine (who wrote "The Age of Reason") was building the first iron bridge in Yorkshire, and Wilberforce and Clarkson were agitating for the abolition of the black slave trade. Thus grew the era of iron and steam. There were now in the north 163 water-mills, 550 mule-jennies of 50 spindles each, and 20,000 hand-jennies of 80 spindles each, all used in the cotton manufacture. In 1789 the French Revolution flared; in 1790 Paine issued "The Rights of Man"; while hand-workers were suffering greatly from the introduction of machinery, and villages were growing into manufacturing towns. From

1790 to 1802 our Continental neighbours were so busy fighting amongst themselves or against Napoleon that they had no time to follow the peaceful domestic arts, so England took this opportunity to become "the workshop of the world," selling to foreigners the goods they had not time to spin or weave for themselves, and thus laying the foundations of that commercial supremacy which is now her greatness, and her glory, and her shame.   That little cock-o'-the-walk Corsican, Napoleon, is therefore, amongst other things, indirectly responsible for the modern factory system, and perhaps it is not the least of the evils that may be laid to his account.   But England, while making goods for the Continent, did not consider how they were being made ; how little children were being worked day and night in order to keep up the supply of yarn. Kings make war, but the people pay for it ; and the women and little children suffer most of all. Mr Gibbins in his "Industrial History of England," thus describes some of the early horrors of the apprentice system,—"English slavery" he calls it. "The manufacturers wanted labour by some means or other, and they got it.   They got it from the workhouses, they sent for parish apprentices from all parts of England, and pretended to apprentice them to the new employments just introduced.   The mill-owners systematically communicated with the overseers of the poor, who arranged a day for the inspection of pauper children.   Those chosen by the manufacturers were then conveyed by wagons or canal boats to their destination, and from that moment were doomed to slavery.

"Sometimes regular traffickers would take the place of the manufacturer, and transfer a number of children to a factory district, and there keep them, generally in some dark cellar, till they could hand them over to a mill-owner in want of hands, who would come and examine their height, strength, and bodily capacities, exactly as did the slave-dealers in the American markets. After that the children were simply at the mercy of their owners, nominally as apprentices, but in reality as mere slaves, who got no wages, and whom it was not worth while even to feed or clothe properly, because they were so cheap, and their places could be so easily supplied. It was often arranged by the parish authorities, in order to get rid of imbeciles, that one idiot should be taken by the mill-owner with every twenty sane children. The fate of these unhappy idiots was even worse than that of the others. The secret of their final end has never been disclosed, but we can form some idea of their awful sufferings from the hardships of the other victims to capitalist greed and cruelty. Their treatment was most inhuman, the hours of their labour were only limited by exhaustion after many modes of torture had been unavailingly applied to force continued work. Children were often worked *sixteen hours* a day, by day and by night. Even Sunday was used as a convenient time to clean the machinery. The author of the 'History of the Factory Movement' writes, 'In stench, in heated rooms, amid the constant whirling of a thousand wheels, little fingers and little feet were kept in ceaseless action, forced into unnatural activity by blows from the heavy hands and feet of the merciless over-looker, and the infliction of bodily pain by instruments of punishment invented by the sharpened ingenuity of insatiable selfishness.' They were fed upon the coarsest and cheapest food, often with the same as that served out to the pigs of their master. They slept by turns, in relays, in filthy beds which were never cool, for one set of children were sent to sleep in them as soon as the others had gone off to their daily or nightly toil. There was often no discrimination of sexes; and disease, misery, and vice grew as in a hotbed of contagion. Some of these miserable beings tried to run away. To prevent their doing so, those suspected of this tendency, had irons riveted on their ankles, with long links reaching up to their hips, and were compelled to work and sleep in these chains, young women and girls as well as boys suffering this brutal treatment. Many died, and were secretly buried at night in some desolate spot, lest people should notice the number of graves; and many committed suicide. The catalogue of cruelty and misery is too long to recite here. It may be read in the 'Memoirs of Robert Blincoe,' himself an apprentice, or in the pages of the

Blue-Books of the beginning of this century, in which even the methodical, dry, official language is startled into life by the misery it has to relate. It is perhaps not well for me to say more about the subject, for one dares not trust merely to try and set down calmly all that might be told about this awful page in the industrial history of England. I need only remark, that during this period of unheeded and ghastly suffering in the mills of our native land, the British philanthropist was occupying himself with agitating for the relief of the very largely imaginary woes of negro slaves in other countries. The spectacle of England buying the freedom of black slaves by riches drawn from the labour of the white ones, affords an interesting study for the cynical philosopher."[1]

John Wesley noticed the phenomenal growth of riches amongst the mill-owners, and tersely recorded his opinion of it in his diary. While visiting Rochdale in 1787 he says: "Invited to breakfast at Bury by Mr Peel, calico printer, who a few years ago began with £500, and is now supposed to have gained £50,000. *Oh, what a miracle, if he lose not his soul!*" We may also say of England, then making itself the richest country in the world, "*Oh, what a miracle, if it lose not its soul!*" Yet 'tis only too evident that England was losing its soul while it was gaining gold.

[1] "Industrial History of England," pp. 178-181.

Out of this state of things naturally arose movements of reform; the workers were forced to make some endeavour to protect themselves; and they began to combine in the secret societies, afterwards known and legalised (in 1824) as trade unions.   Also about this time began the tendency towards what is called Socialism, started by Robert Owen, the real founder of the co-operative system. Also, when steam and machinery came, the poets, who are always prophets and teachers, if they be poets at all, seeing with alarm that man was setting about deforming all his green fields into grey towns, began to try to sing him back to the love of Nature.   Burns, Shelley, Wordsworth, Byron—the former three especially—deplored and denounced the destroying greed of man in many sweet songs to lure him back from gold to God.

In 1794, Mrs Inchbald, an actress of good wit and better heart, wrote her little story of "Nature and Art," satirising the shams and hypocrisies of social and religious life—a little novel that is better worth reading than ninety per cent. of the fiction published to-day.

And still invention toiled and triumphed.   The telegraph was invented, and first established in 1796 (the year when Burns died).   In this year, too, Dr Perceval, a Manchester physician, gave evidence before a Parliamentary Committee at Manchester, on the evil state of the cotton factories, and the brutal treatment of the apprentice children.

In 1798 the London *Times* was printed on the first iron press (invented by the Earl of Stanhope); in 1801 a steamboat sailed on the Thames; in 1802 Greathead invented the lifeboat.

Factories were being built everywhere, and the bad conditions under which the workers were employed had grown so much worse that even Parliament was pressed to interfere, and the Act for the Preservation of Health and Morals was passed in 1802; the very year in which Dr Jenner received £30,000 from the Government for his scheme of vaccination against small-pox. Four years previously, in 1798, the Rev. M. Malthus, seeing the misery already grown big in the growing towns, published his celebrated essay on "The Law of Population," advising "checks" to prevent increase of population, which, he contended, was the chief cause of poverty. But he was wrong; for while the poor were starving their masters were making colossal fortunes out of the new machinery and manufactures. There was ample wealth for everybody; but it was unjustly apportioned.

Robert Owen thus describes the factory population in 1802: "They lived in habits of vice, poverty, and destitution. Thieving was general. Yet the workpeople themselves were systematically opposed to every change I proposed." (Alas! the latter is only too true to-day.)

Quickly came more inventions. In 1804 the power-loom was invented by Cartwright, parson, poet, and philosopher. London was first lit by gas in 1807; steamboats came into use in 1811 (the year King George's son was appointed Regent because his father had gone out of his mind); in 1812, when Napoleon made his black and bitter retreat from Moscow, losing nearly all his army, Jacquard invented the loom that bears his name.

And still the poets strove to sing men back to Nature. What is called the "Poetry of Nature" in our literature began about the same time as the factory system. This may be merely a coincidence; it may be something more. Burns, Wordsworth, Shelley, were all in full song at this period. Robert Bloomfield was writing his poetry of the poor (1798), and Robert Southey had published his revolutionary "Wat Tyler" and his pathetic little poem, "Why the Poor Complain." Also at this time the doctrines of Swedenborg, the seer, were taking hold in the north, Sam. Crompton (the inventor of the spinning-mule, and real founder of Lancashire's trade) being a firm believer in Swedenborg's visions and teachings.

So went the years on, and big history and little history—the former glorious with wars, and kings, and prime ministers, and doings of governments, the latter obscure with the humble lives of oppressed and perishing toilers—was being made. The nominal union between England and Ireland had been effected by Act of Parlia-

ment in 1801; the British were pushing themselves into the land of the Pharaohs and Pyramids;
England, determined to have foreign markets
for her goods, got into wars abroad. Nelson
defeated the French fleet at Alexandria, and the
Danish fleet off Copenhagen; while Napoleon
was subduing the Continent into a peace of fear.
Then, shortly after the execution of poor Robert
Emmett, the Irish patriot, came the startling news
that Napoleon intended to invade England, and
the British yeomanry and volunteer forces were
largely increased. While this was going on at
home, Wellington was winning most of India
for England with his sword, and preparing the
way for more foreign markets. In 1804 Napoleon
was proclaimed Emperor of France; the following
year Nelson defeated the French fleet in the
famous fight off Cape Trafalgar, when the navy's
darling issued that memorable message to his men,
"England expects every man to do his duty," and
met his death in the very moment of triumph.
In fact, at this time, England had fighting going
on in almost every part of the globe, either on
land or sea; and was securing the honours and
the spoils on nearly every occasion. And though
we feel proud of the fighting strength of England,
yet we must also record that the country, taxed to
the utmost to pay for all this fighting, suffered
sore; the poor, of course, most of all; wherefore
there was discontent in the land, and clamour
for justice and reform; followed by suppression

of working-class agitations, culminating in the foul
Peterloo Massacre at Manchester in 1819, when
an inoffensive demonstration was charged by
cavalry.

During this period (wherein Charles Dickens
was born), Charles Lamb was writing his tenderly
humorous essays, and Ebenezer Elliott, afterwards
renowned as "The Corn-Law Rhymer," was
beginning to tread the paths of verse.

Champions of the poor were arising, and others
being born, and these, greater than kings and
generals, started the agitations that have won
reforms which have made the British working-
classes the best-off in the world, though there is
plenty room for improvement yet.

In 1822, a year after the first iron steamship
had been built by Horsley Co., Stafford, our first
cotton twist was exported to India, and the
wealthy began to wear cotton goods. The efforts
of the workers' leaders at last secured the repeal
of the Combination Laws (1824), and trade unions
were first legally permissible in 1825; but their
powers were very limited for many years afterwards. In 1827 the first telegraph was opened
between Liverpool and Holyhead.

The factory system had now grown extensively,
and the oppression of the children in these
spinning dens was so cruel that Oastler, "the
factory king," Sir Robert Peel, Lord Ashley,
and others were stirred into sympathy, and tried
to move the country to do something. This was

in the year 1830, when Roberts invented the
self-acting mule, which was to develop the cotton-
spinning industry as much as Crompton's original
mule; when steel plates and steel pens were
invented; when the first railway (between Liverpool
and Manchester) was opened; when Robert Owen
was experimenting in co-operation; and the police
force was established by Sir Robert Peel (after
whom the constables were nicknamed " peelers ").
In 1831 was passed the First Factory Act; in 1832
the great Reform Bill, to celebrate the passing of
which, Trevethick, the great inventor and dreamer,
proposed to erect an iron structure of which the
Paris Eiffel Tower is but a modern realisation;
and in 1833 the black slave trade was abolished
in the West Indies. But the white slave trade
still went on, for in this very year (1833) Robert
Southey, the poet, wrote, " *The slave trade is mercy
compared to the factory system.*" In this year, also,
trades unions got a little more power.

In 1834 Poor Law Boards were established; in
1835 there were 56,345 little children in 3164
factories; in 1836 Smith invented the first screw
for propelling vessels; in 1837 Queen Victoria
ascended the throne, and Morse's needle telegraph
was invented; and in 1838, when the first steamer
sailed for New York, and photography was
introduced into England, the Chartist movement
began. The following year, 1839, Penny Postage
came into use.

And still the factory system grew, and poverty

B

with it ; and more inventions came. In 1842 the Mining Act prohibited underground pit-work to women in general; in 1843 Tom Hood wrote *The Song of the Shirt*, which, strangely enough, appeared in a comic publication, the Christmas number of *Punch*; O'Connell was agitating in Ireland ; the co-operative movement started in Rochdale in 1844; in 1845 Engels wrote his "Condition of the Working Classes"; in 1846 Howe invented the sewing-machine (which has not yet taken any of the tragedy out of *The Song of the Shirt*), and the electric telegraph was invented ; there were many strikes in the land ; the paper duty was repealed ; and Charles Kingsley was writing his "Christian Socialist" novels—"Yeast," "Alton Locke," "Two Years Ago," etc., just after the great year of revolutions, and the beginning of the modern Spiritualist movement (1848), when the people everywhere rose, or sought to rise, against their rulers. In 1849 the Corn Laws were abolished ; in 1850, while Ernest Jones was urging the lower classes to combine and fight for their rights, Jenny Lind, "the Swedish nightingale," was charming the upper-class world with her voice ; the Menai Tubular Bridge was opened ; and the First Public Libraries Act was passed ; and in 1851 was held the First International Exhibition at the Crystal Palace, as a great peace rejoicing. But the peace was soon broken by the Crimean War (1854), which added £53,000,000 to the National Debt, and was followed by the Indian

Mutiny. In 1856 "Bessemer steel" was first made. In 1859 Darwin published "The Origin of Species," and later (1871) "The Descent of Man" (to prove, as does the factory system, that man is only an extraordinary evolvement from original protoplasmic slime, with much of the ancestral beast still left in him). In 1860, Brown (afterwards Sir John) invented the process for rolling iron plates. Then came the American War, on the abolition of slavery in the United States, 1862 (ten years after the publication of "Uncle Tom's Cabin"), and the terrible "Cotton Panic" in Lancashire (1863), whose woes are described in the poems of Laycock and the prose writings of Waugh and Brierley (three Lancashire writers who have pourtrayed the working-class life of the cotton county in all its phases); since when, until recently, the cotton trade has had its flourishing golden decade, markets being opened up in all parts of the world (by Livingstone in Africa, and other explorers elsewhere). During this period invention had been going on in the woollen trade too. Following Donisthorpe and Lister's wool-combing machine (1840), and Holden's (afterwards Sir Isaac) square-combing machine (1848), Lister, in 1865, discovered how to manufacture plushes from waste. In 1871 the Education Bill—resulting in School Boards—was passed, and trade unions were legalised. In 1872 the Ballot Act was passed. Bell's telephone was invented in 1876, followed by Edison's phonograph (1878).

During this period several good Factory Acts were passed (including the Ten Hours Bill in 1869), and trade unions became great and powerful, while from 1851 to 1881 the number of agricultural labourers in England decreased from 1,253,800 to 870,800,[1] which is significant.

The nineteenth century, it is clear, is the century of invention and growth of manufactures. There have been more inventions during the last hundred years than in all the centuries which have preceded it. And with the growth of manufacture the British Empire has grown greatly. During Queen Victoria's reign (according to *Edinburgh Review*, 1896), we have added 275,000 square miles in India, 80,000 square miles in other parts of Asia; 200,000 square miles in South Africa; and 1,000,000 square miles in East Africa; the British Empire now comprising nearly 10,000,000 square miles.

And here are some figures specially illustrating our progress in mechanical invention. In 1844 a third-class railway ride from London to Exeter took $16\frac{1}{2}$ hours. In 1842 there were 18,000,000 railway passengers; now there are 900,000,000. In 1838 the *Sirius* (700 tons, 320 horse-power), took 18 days from Cork to New York; to-day the *Campania* (12,000 tons, 30,000 horse-power), does the voyage in a little over 5 days. In 1840 our

---

[1] *Land and Labour*, February 1896. In 1891 the number of agricultural labourers had still further decreased to 780,000.

commercial navy totalled 23,000 ships, almost all of wood, total weight, 2,800,000 tons; in 1894 the total was 21,000 vessels, mostly all iron and steel, totalling a weight of 9,000,000 tons, of which 6,000,000 go by steam (fewer vessels now, but much greater in size and total weight).

In 1837 the postage from London to Windsor was 4d.; from London to Edinburgh 13d.; now it is only 1d.

In 1839 the first Annual State Grant to Education was £30,000; now it is £9,000,000.

Now let us see how the cotton trade has grown during the last hundred and fifty years. In 1765 our cotton imports were 3,360,000 lbs.; in 1825, 147,147,000 lbs.; in 1856, 895,115,000 lbs. (spun upon 28,200,000 spindles, averaging 31¾ lbs. per spindle);[1] and in 1894, 1,758,420,512 lbs. (spun upon 40,511,934 spindles,[2] averaging 43½ lbs. per spindle; thus showing that the spindles now spin much more cotton in less hours).

I have thus briefly summarised the chief points and contemporary events in the history of the factory system, in order that the reader may see how the system has grown and developed, and how, since the middle of last century, human progress (in England, anyhow) has all been tending in a mechanical direction, its aim being rather to make money,—the melodramas and novels of the

---

[1] Figures from French's "Life of Crompton."

[2] Figures from "Statistical Abstract," issued by Government.

period corroborate; the hero and heroine are always rewarded in the last scene with a fortune— to make trade, and to manufacture rapidly, than to make a truly happy people living a righteous and rational life.

————

CHAPTER II

THE COUNTRY OF THE COTTON TRADE

I HAVE often wondered why social reformers do not give more attention to Lancashire. Lancashire is "the workshop of the world," to quote an expression which is a poor attempt to hide the prosy horror of the county under a shoddy simile that sounds like poetry; but a workshop is generally not a nice place to live in. Lancashire carries England on its back, is the beast of burden for Britannia. The ass is groaning and tottering now; but of this woe we will treat later.

Put Lancashire right and you put England right. Settle the factory system, and you solve the social problem of the century. Cause Lancashire to smile, and England will be merry. Wash the drooping Red Rose, clear the soot off its polluted petals, give it more soil and more fresh air to grow in, and when the flower of Lancashire is once more blooming in healthy beauty England will become a flourishing garden of delight. Down-trodden, neglected, despised drudge,—Lancashire. A fair and goodly land, ruined by smoke and steam, by a

madness of town-making; its people degenerated
by bad air, by close and impure machine-rooms.
Even as the county itself is ruined by the factory
system, so are its inhabitants; both alike are
blighted and dreary. Yet Lancashire folks were
sturdy men and women once,—the strong hearty
Britons of the west. They must have been a
stock of remarkable endurance to have stood four
generations of the factory system, and yet be alive.
Free, and given a chance in clean air to-day, they
would soon be a glorious race again. Even now,
after a hundred years of a cruel body-and-soul-
marring system, many of them look hale and
fresh; not because of the modern factory system
and its benefits, as some people allege, but in
spite of it, and because of the original robustness
of breed that is not yet thoroughly eradicated.

In this Lancashire of the past and present there
is a fruitful theme for story-teller and bard; the
past is weird with legends and superstitions; tales
of battle and blood, haunted halls, goblin crags
and gorges; stories of grim Pendle Hill, where
the famous Lancashire witches rode in the broom-
stick fashion to awful Malkin Tower; mysterious
Pendle Forest, where spectre horsemen and hounds
startled the belated yokel in the dusk of the day and
the dark of the night; of Old Nick's Waterpot, and
the Magic Giant Cow, whose rib of monstrous size
yet astonishes the rustic Fylde; and a thousand other
thrilling or terrible tales—and often highly humorous ones—of boggarts, fairies, ill-fated lovers, and

the Evil One himself. "Master, you never dreamt what a haunted shire you live in. 'Tis a stockful storehouse of dark shreds torn off the cloak of night; a ragshop of patches of mystery stitched into fantastic and gruesome stories with the tangling thread of words; a gallery full of grotesque effigies and caricatures of the invisible. There are elves, and boggarts, and goblins, and fairies, everywhere. Ne'er a leafy lane, or ancient house, or melancholy ruin, or wild marsh, or whistling wood, or blasted tree, or odd piece of Nature anywhere, but hath its spirit of some sort."

Lancashire has indeed a wonderful folk-lore, and as quaint a set of home-made proverbs and pithy sayings as ever human language devised.

And in this once sweet shire the poet Spenser found his early inspiration; George Fox prayed to God, in leathern breeches; on its moorsides John Wesley planted honest Wesleyanism (now sadly emaciated), and started a tribe of lusty singers to the glory of God, whose voices, even after ten decades of factory wear and tear, have not lost all their strength and charm, as our church and chapel choirs yet bear musical witness.

So much, briefly, for the past. The present has quite as much literary material, if not more; and though the goblins and the giants are gone, their successors, in the shape of tormenting machines and devouring mills, are with us to-day. "There are as deep tragedies and as merry comedies in this county of cotton and coal as in any other piece of land under the sky. Hearts can break and souls make mirth even where steam scalds Nature to death and smoke smuts the heavens with horror." Not that Lancashire has not had its story-tellers and singers—and good ones, too. Harrison Ainsworth has brilliantly painted much of its past in attractive, if melodramatic hues; and in our own day, Waugh, Brierley, Laycock, Mrs Gaskell, Mrs Linnaeus Banks, Trafford Clegg, Miss Lahee, and others, have touched our hearts with homely fun and common griefs, and songs that, if not of the highest, are great with the true humour and pathos of life. To their honour, too, Lancashire's lowly poets have always been on the side of the oppressed and suffering, and all alike deplore the spoiling of the shire by the factory system. If only for this trait, they are worthy a blessing and a memorial. For the blighting and blasting of Lancashire by the factory system is pitiful to see. Surely it is possible for the people to get their daily bread without making all this iron fuss, and steamy nuisance, and smoke, and dirt.

We will look at this ruin; we will behold the living desolation. We will see the spectacle of a devastated land and people. We will examine the factory system of the present time, and note its effects.

And, as I write, it seems to me that my pen is a hot, oily spindle, and my ink a horrible mixture of soot and sweat coloured with human blood.

SECTION II

LANCASHIRE AS IT IS AND WAS

Chapter I

A MANUFACTURING TOWN TO-DAY

MORE than one book, and many essays, have given the history of the modern factory system; but, so far as I know, there has been no attempt to chronicle its general effects. There have been, I am aware, articles in magazines and newspapers purporting to describe "life in a cotton mill," and so forth; but those articles have always been written by outsiders, and, as a rule, show only the most favourable aspects of the factory system; elaborate preparations always being made for such writers when visiting mills and workshops. The workers themselves on such occasions hurry to make their machines trim and clean, and sweat to get all the heavy portion of their day's labour done, so that they may stand idly by their looms or spinning-mules; thus deluding their aristocratic visitors into a notion that factory folk have an easy and joyful time of it; though it must be stated, that the toilers perhaps play this false part out of fear of the overseer and his power to discharge them. Not long since one such visitor wrote to the *Pall Mall Gazette*: "Mechanical

ingenuity has been carried to such a pitch that
the machinery employed in the cotton industry
only wants looking after to turn out its own
work.   This supervision demands knack, but not
exactly skill."   This gentleman, who has grasped
such great conclusions from a little visit to a
cotton mill, has been misled, like many others,
in the manner I have indicated.   He has rushed
through a cotton factory, and seen the "hands"
standing idle by their machines for five minutes
—for just the time he was looking at them.

Here, therefore, I will try to describe the
factory system and its effects as I know them;
and, as I intend to write only of what I know,
I shall confine myself mainly to Lancashire,
where the modern factory system began, and is
still in greatest operation.   The inventor who
started its mighty development was born in my
native town; his statue, grimy with the smoke
from the many mills of which he is practically
the builder, stands in the Nelson Square in that
town to-day.[1]   A study of the factory system in
Lancashire is practically a study of it everywhere,
with, perhaps, this difference, that elsewhere the
evils of the system are greater and the ameliora-
tions less.   There is, too, one other reason why
I take the factory system as it exists in the cotton
manufacture.   The cotton trade is almost as large
as all the other textile trades put together.   In

---

[1] Statue of Samuel Crompton, who was born at Firwood,
Bolton, in 1753.

2538 cotton factories [1] there is a total of 40,511,934 spindles for spinning ; 3,992,885 spindles for doubling ; and 615,714 power looms. In the woollen manufacture there are only 494 spinning factories, 124 weaving factories, 895 for spinning and weaving, and 280 for miscellaneous purposes—a total of 1793 factories, with 3,107,209 spindles for spinning, 299,793 spindles for doubling, 61,831 power looms, and a total of 148,729 persons employed. In the worsted manufacture there are 276 spinning factories, 295 weaving factories, 126 for spinning and weaving, and 56 miscellaneous— a total of 753 factories, with 2,402,922 spindles for spinning, 669,328 spindles for doubling, and 67,391 power looms ; employing a total of 148,324 persons. Then there are 125 shoddy factories, employing 4503 persons ; 357 flax factories, employing 107,583 persons ; 105 hemp factories, employing 10,572 persons ; 116 jute factories, employing 44,810 persons ; 623 silk factories, employing 41,277 persons ; 257 hosiery factories, employing 24,838 persons ; 42 hair factories, employing 2583 persons ; 54 elastic factories, employing 3941 persons ; 403 lace factories, employing 16,930 persons ; and 24 cocoa-nut fibre factories, employing 1746 persons. The total number of persons employed in factories of all kinds in the United Kingdom is 1,184,431. Of these, 528,795 [2]

[1] 935 being spinning factories, 990 weaving sheds, and 175 for miscellaneous purposes.

[2] Of whom 320,000 are females.

are employed in cotton mills; and 655,636 in the remainder.[1] The cotton mills, therefore, employ nearly half the persons working in textile factories in the United Kingdom. It is thus clear that a study of the factory system as it exists in the cotton trade is for all practical purposes a study of the whole modern factory system.

Let us first, then, see how the factory system has transformed—or deformed—the face of nature. From miserable Manchester as a centre start for any part of the county, and what do you find? Under smoky skies are dirty huddled towns, linked together by clanking chains of hideous railway, with spaces of sooty grass and blighted trees left between to show that massacred nature once smiled merrily there. Far, far must you ride before you see grass that is green, and, far, far farther before you find those reliable certificates of clean air, the lichens, which only grow where the atmosphere is of unquestionable purity. Everywhere you will find steam hissing and smoke scowling : factories, forges, furnaces, chimneys, coalpit heads, streams fouled by chemical works—these are the bulk of the scenery in the Shire of Smoke.

That is the general aspect of the county. Now, let us take a typical cotton-manufacturing town. We will take Bolton, because I know it best (and, as I said before, I only intend to write of what I

[1] All these figures are taken from the Statistical Abstract for the United Kingdom for 1896, issued by Eyre and Spottiswoode.

know). Let us stand in Bolton Park, which is
like an isle of dingy green in a black sea, the
charm of the place being utterly obscured by the
fact that from whatever part of it you raise your
eyes you meet a prospect of smoky towers. Looking south, we can count nearly 200 tall chimneys,
rising ugly over a mass of brick buildings, that
look as if they had stood for years in a climate
where it rained ink every day. In addition to 152
cotton-spinning firms,[1] there are 17 engineering
firms (three of which are very large concerns),
about 20,000 houses of every sort, from the slum-
hovel to the outskirt villa, 20 Churches of England,
12 Wesleyan sanctuaries, 6 Roman Catholic chapels,
and 73 places of worship in all (one to about every
1500 inhabitants) ; 520 hotels and beerhouses
(including 103 shops with outdoor licence), 200
butchers, 9 coffee taverns, 35 pawnshops, 170
confectioners' shops, 127 fruiterers and green-
grocers, 60 newsagents, 60 bakers, 30 tripe dealers,
85 cloggers, 101 boot and shoe dealers, 78 milliners,
80 doctors, 1 theatre, 2 music-halls (and a number
of singing-rooms in beerhouses), and 560 provision
dealers. You will note that there are almost as
many beerhouses as provision stores ; more soul-
savers than body physicians ; and that, while there
are 520 beerhouses, there are 60 public elementary
schools, and only two public libraries. Of these
schools, 30 are Board Schools, 21 Church of

[1] Employing 12,000 cotton operatives, including 2400 half-
timers (figures given by Mr R. Waddington, Bolton).

England, 6 Roman Catholic, 2 Wesleyan, and
1 Undenominational.   Thus are the physical,
mental, and spiritual wants of the people supplied.
Round the town, within a radius of five or six miles,
there are 750 farmers—mostly mere milk dealers.
Of market gardeners there are practically none.[1]

In this tight-squeezed medley of mud and manufacture, on an area of about three square miles,
over one hundred thousand men, women, and
children have to live and grow as best they can.
In Oldham, which is a town very like Bolton—
Bolton and Oldham being the two chief centres of
the cotton trade; Bolton for fine spinning, and
Oldham for coarse—there is a population of
141,000; 317 mills, and 11½ million spindles;
44 weaving sheds, and 17,000 looms; 6800 operative spinners, 11,000 full-time piecers (assistants
to the spinners), 4000 weavers, 26,000 cardroom
hands, and 1200 half-timers.[2]

These cotton operatives have Saturday afternoon
and Sunday off work each week, and about another
fortnight's total holidays during the year, consisting
of a couple of days at Easter, three or four days in
Whit-week, a few days in August, and two or three
days at New Year.   In Oldham the operatives have
a full week's holiday all at once—the celebrated
"Wakes" week—in August.   But the glory of
these holidays is dimmed by the fact that the

[1] Post Office Bolton Directory for 1890.
[2] Figures supplied by the secretary to the Oldham
Operative Cotton Spinners' Union.

operatives' wages are "stopped" when the factory is, and the workers themselves, out of scraped savings, have to pay to keep their health up for the benefit of their employers.   At a Mutual Improvement Class in connection with a certain Sunday school, the factory young men who were members thereof freely confessed that they saved up money for holidays, for no other purpose but that of recruiting their health in order to keep up at their work during the rest of the year.   They regarded the week's holiday not so much from a pleasure point of view as a business one.   But fully 50 per cent. of the factory operatives are never able to pinch even one week's seaside sojourn out of their " earnings," or one should rather say their " gettings."

Broadly, the whole population of the town may be divided into three castes, and we may base and begin this classification in the cemetery, where it ends.   There are three sorts of graves, as there are three styles of railway carriage; first-class, second-class, and third-class; and probably, on the resurrection morn, the first-class corpses will have the privilege of being first to be raised.   The first caste, consisting of employers, clergymen, solicitors, physicians, tradesmen on a large scale, dwells in wide suburban streets, made respectably natural with a few trees, inhabiting villas, semi-detached and single, shopping at the big stores (in the daytime, having first choice of everything), drinking at the grand hotels, occupying the front seats at the more select concerts, the boxes, and stalls, and dress circle of the theatre, front cushioned seats nearest the pulpit at church or chapel, buying magazines in addition to newspapers, and having pictures, book-cases, and wine-cellars of their own, and often private carriages.

The second caste is composed of the best paid clerks, book-keepers, managers, and the better sort of working folks; they live in streets narrower than those of caste one, have no trees, drink their beer at smaller hotels, buy food and clothes at the smaller stores (or maybe the Co-operative Society), use the pit of the theatre, the middle and rear pews of the church, buy a newspaper or two, have a few cheap pictures on their walls (the inevitable oil-portrait of the head of the family and his spouse), get books from the public library, perhaps buy a few of their own, and walk, or use tram.

The third caste is made up of "labourers" and poorer workmen; they live in small houses,—all joined and jammed together to save space and make more rents for the landlord—in narrow streets; they shop at the smallest and dirtiest shops, they drink in low taverns, we find pawnshops numerous in their localities, they get their music in hideous singing rooms, they sit in the gallery at the theatre, they have no books, no church, no art.

Beneath these there is a fourth caste; but these cannot be classified, for they cannot afford even a bury-hole for cemetery classification. While the first caste awaits righteous resurrection

c

under a grand monument, and the second and third under stone and wooden memorials, the carcases of the fourth caste are dumped and lumped into the "common" graves.

Chapter II

THE SAME TOWN A HUNDRED YEARS AGO

IN 1770 Bolton was a fair hamlet; a hundred years have made it into an ugly town. Its inhabitants to-day would hardly believe their eyes if they saw a picture of Bolton in 1770[1]—a picture of the old Parish Church shown standing on a grassy hill, with the clean river, in which kine, knee-deep, are drinking, flowing by its base; leafy trees and green meads all around; not one factory chimney in the scene. To-day, from that same Parish Churchyard, how different is the prospect!—a fouled river, no trees, no fields, and scores of factory chimneys, with a busy railway close by. All the other South Lancashire towns have been similarly changed.

The population of Bolton in 1770 was about 5000; it is now twenty times that number. It increased rapidly with the development of the factory system, as the following figures show[2]:—

----

[1] There is one—an engraving in a book entitled "The Sayings and Doings of Parson Folds."

[2] From "Sayings and Doings of Parson Folds."

	Population.			Population.
1801.	12,549.		1851.	61,172.
1811.	24,149.		1861.	70,395.
1821.	31,295.		1871.	92,655.[1]
1831.	43,396.		1895.	118,300.[2]
1841.	49,747.			

It was in 1779 that Crompton finished his spinning-mule, which revolutionised the cotton industry; as Crompton's mule multiplied, so did the population of Bolton and of Lancashire.

"In 1753," says French, describing Bolton, "gardens, meadows, and bleaching crofts, dotted here and there with cottages stretched on the north side to the (river) Croal, then a pleasant stream of pure water. . . . There were no tall chimneys in Bolton in these days."[2]   In 1766, "Sweet Green" House, still bearing that name, but now neither green nor sweet of situation, had an orchard where "large and numerous apple and other fruit trees" flourished.[3]   To-day locomotives shriek and roar past "Sweet Green"; opposite its door is the second largest engineering works in the town, full all day, and often night, of the noise of hammers and hissing of steam; the old "sweet green" orchard is a slum; and as for

[1] 1891 Census.   These figures are for Bolton Borough alone, and do not include the townships that are now practically one with the borough — the total population of the district will be above 250,000.

[2] Life of Samuel Crompton, inventor of the spinning-mule.

[3] "Sayings and Doings of Parson Folds."

"apple and other fruit trees," there are none to be found within a very wide radius of Bolton in the present year of our Lord.

Little did poor, noble Samuel Crompton, as he secretly fashioned his invention in Hall-i'-th'-Wood during the years 1775-1779, dream what a change he was going to work—"work" is the fit word—in Lancashire.

Looking at Bolton from the northern moors above Hall-i'-th'-Wood to-day — in Crompton's time a beautiful sylvan spot, very place for a man, not to devise mere cunning mechanism, but poetically to reach "the highest heaven of invention," and even yet a not ugly retreat, though smirched and surrounded with smoke and steam—looking, I say, down on Bolton to-day from this Hall-i'-th'-Wood, where the unobtrusive and well-meaning inventor laboured and schemed so long to perfect the spinning-mule[1] that was to be his own material undoing, but the moneyed making of so many others, and which was to change his native soil from a happy hamlet amid the merrie moors to a mighty manufacturing centre of filth and fume, one beholds a terrible heap of houses and buildings, with blackened church spires standing here and there, and hundreds of high chimneys belching forth, like huge fiery dragons, till the whole place looks like a city sunk in a sea of smoke. Amidst that sickening jerry-jumble of

[1] Crompton's original mule may be seen in the Mere Hall Park Museum, Bolton.

cheap bricks and cheaper British industry, over
a hundred thousand men, women, and children
toil and exist, sweating in the vast, hot, stuffy
mills and sweltering forges; going, when young,
to the smut-surrounded schools to improve their
minds, and trying to commune with the living God
in the dreary, dead, besmirched churches and
grimy puritanical chapels; growing up stunted,
breeding thoughtlessly, dying prematurely, knowing
not, nor dreaming, except for here and there
a solitary one cursed with keen sight and sensitive
soul, of aught better and brighter than this shriek-
ing, steamy sphere of slime and sorrow.

Modern Bolton is the direct outcome of the
factory system. Its inhabitants know little of
flowers, and less of birds. Its children do not
know the joy of the fields, the glory of the grass,
the beauty of the trees; they think that land is
only to build factories and houses upon; that
while it is doing nothing but grow vegetation,
it is wasted. The parents would laugh if told
that the real waste of the land began when cotton
mills were planted upon it. Their eyes see
nothing very hideous or sad in their town; they
have been used to nothing better. In fact, it is
only recently that I myself saw fully what a
horrible place a manufacturing town is. From
my birth till the age of thirty I lived in such
a town—in fact, in Bolton itself—then, by rare
luck, I came to dwell by the sea, in the Fylde,
the Garden of Lancashire (for there are two

distinct Lancashires, one manufacturing, the other rural), the nearest factory twenty miles away; and I wandered in the fields and on the sandy shore, and, for the first time in my life, had opportunity to enjoy fresh flowers and clean skies and unsmutched verdure. Finding out, with pleasure, the names of the wild flowers and trees I ought to have had chance of knowing years before; learning, too, how to distinguish the wild birds and their songs, which also I ought to have had for delight in my childhood's days, I thought myself in a new world of beauty, and felt like a man born and reared in a prison, then suddenly given liberty in the midst of charming scenery.

And then, when I went back for a brief visit to the cotton town where I was born, I saw it as I never saw it when I dwelt therein. Living there, I had grown familiar with its ugliness, and familiarity oftener breeds toleration than contempt; I had accepted the drab streets, the smoky skies, the foul river, the mass of mills, the sickly workers, as inevitable and usual—nay, natural, and did not notice them in any probing, critical way. But, after a year's absence, I saw, with a shock—ay, and felt and tasted—the dismal horror of it all. I had never realised the greatness of the dreary evil before.

The thick polluted air that gave me a headache, the soot that fell on me and stuck in my eyes as I walked the streets, the grim monotony of everything—now I knew, and shuddered, having known better and sweeter things; and I said that I would rather die than live in such a hell again, remembering, in agony, as I thus vowed, the brothers and sisters and friends doomed till death to that torment, and for whom I could do nothing but tell the truth of their fate to the world.   My wife, herself a factory lass, who had all her life hitherto seen nothing very dreadful in town existence, was now, like me, filled with loathing and repugnance, and pity; while our little girl and boy, aged respectively four and three, having seen nothing of this before as their parents had, said, pleadingly, "This is a dirty place; let us go back to the sea and the grass."

Such was the effect that Bolton—which is undoubtedly one of the best-looking and most sanitary of all Lancashire manufacturing towns—had on me, after living in it thirty years, leaving it, and then visiting it after a twelvemonth's absence.

And it will be a good day for the inhabitants of Bolton when they see their town as now I see it, and a happy thing for England, if, after realising the ugliness of their town, they set about mending and beautifying it by undoing it.   The same may be said of every other Lancashire manufacturing town, with this addition, that most of them are much worse-looking than Bolton.

Yet, for the enlightenment of those who may object to the preceding statements as mere sentimental imagining and exaggerated fancy, we will, in succeeding chapters, get full proof of these assertions from men of fact and practicality.

SECTION III

THE UNHEALTHINESS OF THE FACTORY SYSTEM

CHAPTER I

DEATH RATES

PERHAPS I had better say, at the outset of this chapter, that I admit that Lancashire has improved in some things this last fifty years (though, in my opinion, many of the "improvements," which would never have been necessary but for the evils made by the factory system, are merely attempts to set things right again after first putting them wrong). The condition of the working classes is better in some respects. The factory system has been rendered less evil by slow legislation, long struggled for, and only obtained by fierce fighting.[1] Educational facilities are increased; the sanitation of the towns is much better; amusements and recreations are multiplied; hours of toil are lessened; food, clothes, books, papers, and railway travelling are cheaper.

[1] For full particulars of factory legislation see Plener's "History of Factory Legislation," and Cooke-Taylor's "The Factory System and Factory Acts."

And so is human flesh and blood. On the other hand, the labour in the cotton factories is harder, more worrying, owing to the greater speed of the machinery; the swelling numbers of unemployed make it difficult for a man to get in work again when once thrown out; the struggle for existence under individualistic conditions has become keener and keener, as not alone the workers but dwindling tradesmen and even pinched middlemen can testify out of their troubles.

Let us see how the factory system of to-day differs from that of half-a-century ago. Here are the improvements, gains, etc., set side by side with the present state of things:—

PROGRESS.	THE PRESENT—*Contra.*
Age of half-timers raised from 8 to 11 years. Age of full-timers from 13 to 14.	Cram in schools and Code torture of half-timers. Many accidents to children in factories.
A certain stage of educational proficiency to be reached before a child may go to work in the mill.	Greater speed of improved machinery, whereby the work is increased six-fold, resulting in physical deterioration and mental worry.
Improved lighting, sanitation, and ventilation in factories.	Married women working up to very day of confinement.
Hours of labour reduced for half-timers to 6½ hours per day; for adults to 10 hours per day, or 56½ hours per week.	Increase of unemployed in cotton trade; increase in size of already too large overcrowded, ugly towns; slums; increase of death-rate; sickly, stunted population; fretting precariousness of employment; increase of pauperism in Lancashire.
Protection against dangerous machinery.	
Increased holidays.	
Greater factory supervision by inspectors.	
Sundry Education Acts. Employers' Liability Acts. Artisans' Dwellings Acts.	

And, briefly put, here is the indictment against the factory system : It is unhealthy, dangerous, bad for mind and morals, has an injurious effect on family life, unfits women for motherhood, curses the children, and is causing the people of Lancashire to deteriorate.

First, as to the unhealthiness. I take figures from the Report of the Medical Officer of Health for Lancashire for the year 1896 (issued November 1897,—this book was begun in 1895), and from " Annual Summary of Births, Deaths, etc., in London and other large Towns," for 1896 (issued in 1897 by the Registrar-General for England. These figures show that the death-rate of the Lancashire towns greatly exceeds that of the rural and seaside districts in the county. Here they are, side by side :

DEATH-RATES
(ANNUAL RATE PER 1000)

LANCASHIRE FACTORY TOWNS.		LANCASHIRE RURAL DISTRICTS.	
Manchester	25·65	Blackpool	13·8
Salford	25·46	Lytham	10·7
Oldham	20·27	Southport	13·1
Blackburn	17·87	Carnforth	9·6
Bolton	23·49	Turton	10·6
Burnley	20·11	Eccles	13·0
Preston	22·82	Grange	9·2
Wigan	23·8	Little Crosby	6·2
Ashton	21·2	Little Woolton	5·8
Rochdale	20·2	Morecambe	11·3
Stockport	20·7	St Anne's	7·3
Bury	20·1	Whitworth	12·0
		Withnell	11·1

The death-rate of Liverpool (whose size is largely due to the cotton trade) is 24·97. The death-rate for London is, on the average, 18 per 1000. It is curious to note, by the way, that the population of Bolton is denser in proportion to area than any town in the kingdom, except London and Plymouth. In Bolton, there are 51 persons to the acre; in Manchester, only 41; while for London and Plymouth, the figures are respectively, 59 and 58 persons per acre.

But to get the best proof of the unhealthiness of factory life, one needs but stand near the gates of one of the spinning or weaving establishments in any cotton town when the workers are leaving for dinner, or at the end of the day's toil. The spinners or minders are all pale, generally hollow-chested, and troubled with bronchial complaints. The weavers (mostly women and girls) are blood-less of face, round-shouldered, and have always bad teeth (caused by sucking the weft up in the shuttle). The cardroom lasses are sallow, and afflicted with chest complaints through inhaling the cotton dust. The young children are bleached of countenance, or in process of bleaching; you will find them in various stages, according to the length of time they have been employed in the factory. Especially on a bleak winter's day, when the factory hands quit the hot mill (arti-ficially heated to over 90 degrees for the purposes of manufacture), and come out into the chilly damp air (which is a natural aid to spinning)[1] are the effects of their close confinement noticeable.

CHAPTER II

A FACTORY DAY AND FACTORY WORK

LET us see under what conditions the factory operatives live and labour; let us see what one of their working-days is like. We will take a winter's morning at 5 A.M. Dark the desolate streets, dark the silent houses and shuttered shops, dark and soundless the huge factories and sombre weaving-sheds, dark the forsaken public squares and places, dark the empty schools and solemn churches and stiff chapels, dark now the hotels and beershops, and hushed their tipsy din, dark the tombstoned cemetery and withered public park, dark all heaven and earth, save for the far-off stars fixed above, and the lonely gas-lamps set at certain distances by man in the dreary world below, — the manufacturing town of Spindleton at 5 o'clock on a cold December morning. There is nothing human about this early darkness of a winter's morning—this darkness that is not the welcome close of a day's toil, but the strange drowsy darkness that lies at the

---

[1] A moist climate is best for the cotton manufacture ; the climate of Lancashire is equal to 7 per cent. in the cost of production.

wakening end of sleep and dreams, and is con-
fused with thoughts of waiting work and day
beginning,—no revellers' cabs rattling late through
the stony solitude; no benighted drunkard lurch-
ing home with guttural noise; no fond lovers
lingering and kissing night away at the gable
corner. Somewhere, unseen, policemen are going
their rounds through the still streets; occasionally
a furnace flame leaps up like some fiery goblin
from one or other of the great ironworks;
sometimes a far-off metal clang and clamour is
faintly heard, as if demons were working while
men slept; here and there, on the outskirts of
the black block of huddled houses and mills, a
distant brick-kiln glows weirdly red through the
gloom. "But hark! The hideous steam
buzzers (whistles) are beginning to shriek. The
knockers-up (persons engaged to rouse the
workers) are busy rattling at the bedroom
windows with their long poles; the toilers surlily
jump up and tap back at the pane growling,
'What, time to get up awready? I'm sure I've
nobbut just come to bed. Eh, I could do wi'
just another turn o'er!' They rise, spluttering
about in the dark, shivering as they stick their
legs into icy trousers and skirts, and wishing all
the factories were at the bottom of the sea. In
a few minutes the streets will be full of the great
glum procession hurrying to the mills and workshops. The town is getting up to its work; the
older folks grumbling at having to rise, and

the younger ones being literally dragged out of bed."

We stand in the midst of thick streets. Now, "the patter of a pair of wooden clogs is heard a short distance off; then another patter down a street to the right, followed by another down a street to the left. Then, almost in an instant, it seems, the great, dark, hard silence begins to rattle with the sharp clatter, clatter, clatter of thousands of clogs—with here and there the shoes of an overseer, or higher-grade artisan—in which are the feet of the working-men and women and children, who are hastening to the spinning-factory, weaving-shed, and foundry, with surly aspect, mutely protesting at the fate that thus forces them unseasonably from bed; and with bowed heads drawn down into their necks, arms tightly pressed to their sides, hands deep in pockets (or under their shawls in case of females), as if trying to squeeze their bodies into as little compass as possible to be exposed to the chill, raw air." In the semi-lit gloom you cannot see the worn, ghastly faces of the men and women, nor the tired eyes of the shivering half-time lads and lasses; but we shall see them later on.

"Next the lights begin to pop out in the cottages, not to be lit again till the wives at home arise an hour or so later to make the breakfasts to send (often by the younger children) to the fathers and husbands and sons and daughters now beginning their day's work with the spindles

and shuttles. The shops and offices of the
borough are still in undisturbed darkness, for the
tradesmen and solicitors and clerks and others
of a caste above manual labour, have not to quit
bed till two hours after the working-classes ; while
the still more superior gentry, the merchants, and
manufacturers, and larger employers, will show
their importance by not getting to business till an
hour or two after the shopkeepers' assistants have
taken the shutters down from the plate glass
windows."

We walk on with the sullen throng, and pass
"a steaming coffee-can, standing under the flare
of a paraffin-lamp, on a wooden stall fixed outside
the window of a small house. At this stall such
cotton operatives as desire a warm drink, and
have the time and money to afford for a short
pause, stop and purchase a pot of coffee." As a
rule, the workers, if they do not put off their
rising till the last minute, get a drink of tea at
home ere setting out for work, leaving the tea-pot
in the oven overnight.

The minutes speed on towards six o'clock. The
procession begins to thin. Big batches of it are
disappearing into the factories and forges. A
few more minutes, and "the rapid clatter of
clogs has ceased as suddenly and strangely as it
began. The streets are again as quiet as at mid-
night. But there is a difference. Bodies and
souls, both poor and oppressed alike, have flitted
through the streets in the interval. Now the giant

mills are all aglow from cellar to roof, and the
wheels of engine and spinning-room and weaving-
shed begin to stir the silence with buzzing sound,
and the hum of machinery fills the gloomy air."

That is a description of the factory operative's
early morning rise and march to work in bleak
winter.   In summer, of course, the conditions are
changed somewhat for the better; snow and
chilly rain and freezing cold are absent.   But
the early rising, the trudge breakfastless to the
mill are there always, in every season.   And,
whether he be in the humour or not, or a little
out of sorts with headache or other ailment, the
factory operative must rise and tramp off to his
toil.   If he be four or five minutes late the factory
gate is shut against him, and his week's wages
are less by "a quarter" of a day's pay.   And if
he be often late he goes some day to find his
place filled, and his occupation gone.

Now, what is the work inside the mill?   In big
rooms full of wonderfully complicated machinery,
we behold the factory operatives, male and female,
now having doffed the clothes in which they left
their homes, and attired in their factory costume,
which is, in the men's case, as little costume as
possible.   The spinners (males) are clad only in
shirt, with sleeves rolled up, and a pair of thin
white drawers, reaching to the ankles, and are
bare-footed (for shoes or clogs would slip on the
oil-saturated wooden floor); the female weavers
and cardroom lasses wear a short skirt, having

taken off their shawls and dresses and hats. The hair is also tied up, as there is danger of it catching in the machinery. The "piecers" (boys and youths) are dressed as lightly as the men, and are also in bare feet.

The factories start at 6 o'clock A.M., and stop at 8 till 8.30 for breakfast, which is generally taken in the mill, as the time is too brief for the operatives to put on their clothes and go home. Then the machinery rattles away again till 12.30 when an hour is allowed for dinner. Those who do not live far go home to dinner; but many are forced to have this meal also in the mill. At 1.30 the engine starts again, and does not stop till 5.30, when the day's work is done. On Saturday the work finishes at 1 o'clock, giving the operatives Saturday afternoon for holiday.

The toil is ceaseless; the machinery demands constant watching. Once on a time this was not so; the machinery ran slowly, and the operatives had a fair amount of leisure in the factory. But all that is altered and abolished to-day. As I have said before, the production in cotton mills has increased without corresponding increase of hands, showing that machinery has largely superseded human labour, and that the machinery runs much quicker too. "From the first second of entering the factory in a morning to the last turn of the wheels in an evening the operatives have no rest. Their feet are never still; their hands are full of tasks; their eyes

D

are always on the watch; they toil in an unend-
ing strain that is cruel on the nerves. The glory
of their occupation is gone; the days when their
labour was not a weary burden are over; now
it is all hot rush and ceaseless worry; in sad
sweating and groaning the people scratch their
bits of corn out of the hard days."

Try to picture what these spinners (or self-act
minders) and weavers have been doing unceasingly
from 6 o'clock in the morning till half-past 12
at noon, with only a thirty minutes interval for
breakfast—often shortened to twenty-five or twenty
minutes by the employers' "cribbing"—*i.e.* running the engine late, and starting it sooner than
the legal time, which is almost done daily unless
the factory inspector chance to be about.

For six hours the male spinner has been standing in the midst of 2500 whirling spindles, every
thread of which must be incessantly watched by
himself and two assistants, so that it may be
instantly "pieced up" if it break, in a hot room,
amid machinery roaring so loudly that one can
only converse with those close at hand, and only
then at the top of one's voice, amid whizzing
wheels, and bands, and swift-straps, which would
snatch off a limb for a second's carelessness; all
this in hot air, so hot that in summer a great thirst
scorches the throat; and for the same length of
time the female weaver has been encircled by four
clattering looms, with shuttles making 200 or more
picks per minute, in a "steamed" atmosphere;

and a din even worse than that of the spinning-room, and in which a deaf and dumb method of communication has to be used; while at any instant a rebellious shuttle may shoot forth and knock an eye out (I have myself frequently met young women who were thus blinded at their work), or a loose skirt may be seized by wheel or strap, and then—horror!

And all these hours—ten hours a day—spinner and weaver are on their feet: no sitting down; no resting; one must keep up to the machinery though agonised with headache, or troubled by any other complaint. While the engine runs the workers must stand: the machinery cares nought for fatigue, weakness, ailment, sorrow, anxiety for sick husband, wife, or child, at home; grief for a dear one's recent death, maybe the night before; with the motion of the spindles and shuttles no human pain or woe must interfere: the workers must leave all their heart and soul at home when they go to the factory. All they need is "hands," and brains sufficient to guide the "hands" and keep the body out of danger. Sometimes the torture is worse than that of a treadmill; one *must* keep the pace, or—but there is no alternative. Once on a time, as just stated, ere the speed of the machinery was accelerated to the present pitch, the spinners had time for a chat, and even a nap at their work; while the weavers could snatch pages of reading from a book, or do knitting or sewing; but not so to-day. In some places they

are even "timed" when using the "conveniences";
and only allowed so many minutes for nature's
necessity, being fined if exceeding the limit fixed.

Thirty years ago, in 1866, Mr Philip Grant, in
his "History of Factory Legislation," says, concerning the distance walked daily by spinners and
piecers in following the mule-carriage, "I found
that the distance was not less than 20 miles in 12
hours. This was on slow machinery. On quicker
machinery it was 30 miles in the same time." To-
day it is much more.

It will thus be seen that this employment is a
severe and ceaseless mental strain that makes a
tribe of toilers alert at their tasks, but weakens
the physique, as does all narrow and monotonous
mental strain, if continuous. For only one part
of the brain is used; that is, the observing faculty
at the expense of all the rest; for, in the midst
of such lightning machinery, there is no time for
reflection; everything must be quick — instant
action. Thus, probably, the other faculties are
overdrawn upon to sustain the strain upon the
observing faculty, which physiologically and
psychologically accounts for the inability of the
average cotton operative to exercise his other
mental functions.

1. Allen Clarke, *Teddy Ashton*, as a young man in 1896.

2. Young ring spinners, Barne's no 3 Mill Farnworth,
about 1915.

3. The Little Piecer, an Oldham Mill about 1900.

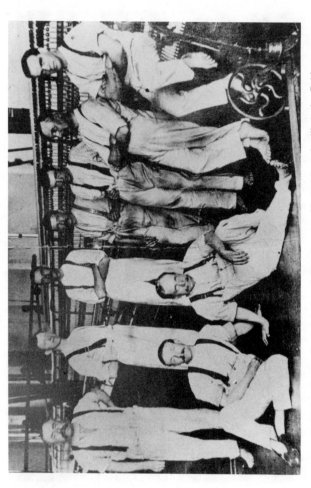

4. Mule spinners ("minders") and side piecers at Hesketh's no 3 mill, Astley Bridge, Bolton about 1910.

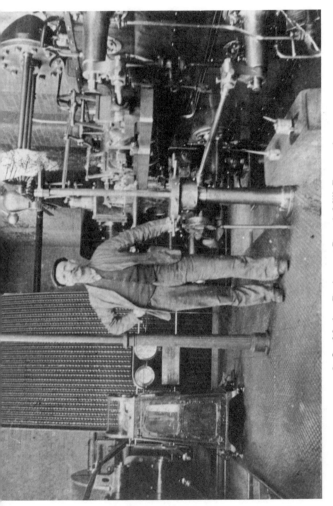

5. Joe Markey, Engineer at Barne's Mill, Farnworth.

Arden Street

6. Homes fit for heroes? Arden Street, Halliwell in the 1920s.

Deansgate, Bolton

7. Edwardian Deansgate, Bolton, from postcard about 1905.

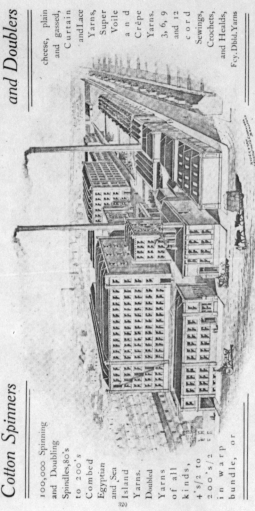

THOMAS TAYLOR & SONS, LTD.,

GRECIAN MILLS, LEVER ST.,
BOLTON.

Cotton Spinners
and Doublers

100,000 Spinning
and Doubling
Spindles, 80's
to 200's
Combed
Egyptian
and Sea
Island
Yarns.
Doubled
Yarns
of all
kinds,
4's/2 to
200's/2
in warp
bundle, or

cheese, plain
and gassed,
Curtain
and Lace
Yarns,
Super
Voile
and
Crêpe
Yarns.
3, 6, 9
and 12
cord
Sewings,
Crochets,
and Healds,
Fcy. Dbld. Yarns

320

Telegraphic Address:
"ACORN, BOLTON."

Telephone No.:
31 BOLTON.

8. Advertisement c. 1900. Taylors spun some of the world's finest yarns.

CHAPTER III

DISEASE AND DEBILITY OF FACTORY OPERATIVES

WHAT wonder then, that, after such wearying, worrying days, continued from year to year, coupled with having to live in packed streets and vitiated air after leaving work, the cotton operations are not healthy.

But it may be alleged that the factory is not the chief cause of this mental and physical debility. Here, then, is medical evidence [1]—

Dr Sergeant (Preston), medical officer for Lancashire, says:—"The conditions which surround persons employed in the cotton mills of this county (Lancashire) deserve careful consideration, and it would be desirable to know to what extent the health of the hands is endangered. It seems to be admitted that the high temperature of the mills, combined with an abnormal humidity of the air produced by 'steaming' (done by the manufacturer to make bad material weave easier) tends to diminish in the workers the power of resisting disease, more especially of a pulmonary character. The humid atmosphere promotes perspiration, but makes evaporation from the skin more difficult, and as a result the underclothing becomes

[1] Chest complaints are common in all the manufacturing towns. In Bolton, during 1896, there were 2492 deaths from all causes; 588 being due to disease of the respiratory organs, and 365 to constitutional disease (probably of a respiratory character).

moistened. In this condition the operative, when he leaves the mill, and has to face a much-reduced temperature, is most liable to take cold, which may be the forerunner of some serious chest affection." [1]

Dr Sergeant also draws attention to the smoke nuisance ; especially in Ashton-under-Lyne and other manufacturing towns. He says : " From my own knowledge of the subject I would safely advise Sanitary Authorities not to allow more than five minutes' black smoke from the chimney of any factory furnace in one hour without interference, and such would only be fair to the inhabitants of the borough from a sanitary point of view without being exacting to the manufacturers." [2] In my own opinion, five minutes' black smoke per hour, for a day of ten hours, from 200 chimneys, would be rather too much for the health of the people dwelling in the thick of it ; but, of course, one must not be too exacting on the manufacturers, who, by the way, don't live in the smoke themselves : they only take their money out of it.

Were it not for the injurious toil and sad slavery, a cotton mill would be a splendid monument to man's skill. The marvellous and complex machinery, that seems to work with hands, feet, and eyes, that acts almost as if it had a conscious brain, is startling in the almost human, though automatic, perfection it has reached. And it never makes a mistake. These

[1] Report for 1894. [2] Report for 1894.

iron skeletons with steel arms are not hampered with flesh and stomach, and therefore are not troubled by passions and hunger; they never feel indigestion nor headache; they want no food; they desire no other sex nor children to love; and in all this non-humanness and immunity from mortal perversities their owner no doubt thinks them superior to the living "hands" that needs must indulge their bothersome clay in its wants and instincts, or else prove awkward and intractable. On the other side, while the machines have almost become human, the human tenders of them have almost become machines. Thus has good invention been turned to ill, and the brain set to work against the "hand" instead of for it, causing machines to curse, instead of bless; but of all things that have been misused since the world began, nothing has been worse misused than man—except women and children.

The "steaming" referred to deserves a special paragraph to itself, just to show to what homicidal extent the manufacturers will go in order to cheat buyers and make big profits. I quote from a leading article in the *Factory Times* of February 21, 1896: "It was soon found that by putting in more and more steam the quantity of 'size' which a warp would carry could be increased to an indefinite extent, and as this substitution of china clay—the principal substance used in making the 'size' for cotton yarn—enabled the manufacturer to put his cloth on the market at a much cheaper

rate, there arose a demand for these cheap goods
. . . until the warp became as much adulterant
as yarn. It is, therefore, scarcely surprising to
find some of the weaving sheds of pre-regulation
days were simply hot-beds of disease." In 1889
an Act was passed to remedy this state of things,
but matters are not much better to-day. It looks
as if the masters care not how they endanger the
health and lives of their employés in the quest
after profits.

During the year 1894, respiratory diseases—
bronchitis, pneumonia, and pleurisy — caused
5795 deaths in Lancashire, or one-fifth of the
total mortality. The number of deaths from
respiratory diseases was largest in winter, when
the change from the hot factory to the cold air
outside is the most severe.[1] Here are the
mortality returns from the Registrar-General's
report for the week ending November 16, 1895 :—

Blackburn .	.	.	36 deaths per 1000		
Bolton	.	.	26	,,	,,
Burnley	.	.	21	,,	,,
Liverpool .	.	.	30	,,	,,
Manchester .			22	,,	,,
Oldham	.	.	21	,,	,,
Salford	.	.	25	,,	,,
Preston	.	.	20	,,	,,

In contrast with these the death-rate for London

[1] A total of 1699 in January, November, and December
(figures from Medical Officer's Report).

—packed London—is only 18 per 1000, while the death-rate of the rural districts of Lancashire averages about 10 per 1000.

There is another ever-present proof of the unhealthiness of the Lancashire manufacturing towns. Nowhere will you find so many "quack" doctors and herbalists; nowhere will you find a greater sale of patent medicines and pills. The Lancashire factory operatives hardly ever feel quite well; they are always hanging between moderately bad health and serious illness, mostly troubles of indigestion and chest complaints. Not sufficiently ill to call in the services of a qualified practitioner (which is expensive), they are nearly always ill enough to require dosings of bronchitis mixture, headache pills, etc. Indeed, the factory operatives crawl through a ghastly life of unhealthy workshop decorated with rows of physic bottles and pill-boxes.

The appetites of the factory operatives are always "queer," too. They cannot eat plain food, but must have the sickened appetite coaxed with dainties (a "bit of a taste" as they call it). The quantities of pickles and vinegar sold in Lancashire must be enormous. The factory hand's stomach is so disordered with the close, stuffy, dusty air of the mill, and the shortness of the meal-hour, that only allows time to gulp down food without chewing it, that it cannot take ordinary food unless well seasoned with things that no healthy digestive apparatus ever craves.

The factory operatives are great flesh-eaters. It would seem that their utter severance from the soil by machinery has taken out of them all agricultural instincts and vegetarian likings. Even if they have broth, it must be well filled with chopped beef, or beef in the piece. Working-class mothers are in the habit of giving a piece of beef, or "fleish" as they call it, to very young children, and even babies under twelve months old. I have seen pork-sausage given to children of two and three years of age. Pig—bacon, ham —is extensively eaten. There can be no doubt that this flesh-eating has something to do with making the people carnivorously cruel and selfish, and has its effects on morals as well as health. Of course, the factory folks have no time for vegetable cookery; their short meal-hours won't allow it; besides, the factory atmosphere creates, as I have pointed out, a diseased appetite, which does not care for simple natural food, but runs after seasoned and artificial dishes.

There is no doubt that much of the un-healthiness of factory operatives is caused by the shortness of the meal-hours, and the fact that many of those employed in the cotton trade are compelled to eat their food in the mill.

The following article on "The Health of Female Factory Operatives," is taken from the *Factory Times* of February 14th, 1896:—

"Within the past few days our attention has been called to the fact that one of the principal doctors in the town of Huddersfield, whose patients are mainly among the working-classes, has been saying some strong things in regard to the system of factory life, such as it is at the present time. Short of agreeing with all, we certainly agree with most of what he said. In the first place, this gentleman complains that a far greater proportion of operatives whom he has to treat are young people, and these are mostly of the gentler sex. This, to begin with, may partly be accounted for on the ground that of late years there has been a marked difference in some trades as to the proportions of male and female labour. Take weaving only as an example. Formerly there would be in the Huddersfield district about seventy per cent. of men weavers to thirty per cent. of women. To-day, we believe, the percentages are about reversed—at all events, there are not more than forty per cent. of men, if so many. No doubt there are other cases in which women have crept into trades which were formerly occupied by men exclusively or nearly so. Now, weaving is hard work, especially in the woollen trade, and were it not for the fact that women will work for less money many employers would regard their labour in a different light. It is not, however, with this aspect of the question that our medical friend is mostly concerned. If women were well fed they could stand a fair amount of hard work. Are they well fed?

"This is the aspect of the question that the

doctor has been inquiring into, and we believe that he has come to the conclusion that they are far from being in that happy condition. If a mill girl is lucky she may get a cup of warm tea or coffee before starting out of a morning. Generally, however, this is where some other member of the family gets up and prepares it. Cases will oftener happen when the other member of the family has to get to work half-an-hour or an hour sooner than the girls. This cup of tea is usually taken without any solid food. Such nourishment, or stimulant, has to cover a walk of from five to thirty minutes possibly, and, after reaching work, until breakfast-time. The breakfast consists, say, of a cup of tea and a slice, or, at the outside, two slices of bread and butter. This is frequently taken in some quiet corner of the room, where four or five may be found sitting on the floor or any basket or low stool there may be about. Remember, also, that dust, dirt, and grease are flying about whilst meals are being taken. In some instances the shafting may be going, but as this, we believe, is contrary to the law, the point need not be laboured. Of course, there are some firms where dining-rooms are provided, but these are frequently so dirty in regard to walls, roofs, and ceilings as to be almost as bad as the rooms in which the operatives work.

"When breakfast is over the operatives must go at it again until dinner-time, when, of course, the ordinary outsider might think that the operatives would see about having meat and potatoes and pudding, or some such fare. That is far from a picture of actual facts. In hundreds, nay thousands of instances, the operative gets a repetition of the breakfast menu, with perhaps a slight variation, including a little meat in the shape of a sandwich, or bread and jam. Very often this is taken in the loom-gate, or in a corner of the mill: and thus the days go along, and from year end to year end this miserable round of tea and bread and butter, and butter and bread and tea, goes on. When it is considered that very many of these girls will be the future mothers of England, no wonder that medical men are beginning to cry out that it is time for a change. In the first place, all operatives, for dining purposes, ought to be compelled to vacate rooms where work is carried on. Secondly, employers might with advantage permit someone to cook for the workpeople, and prepare any food that operatives may choose to bring. The inspectors also ought to have power to fine work-people or employers if the former are caught taking meals in the mill. We are glad that even one medical man is taking this important matter up, and we trust that he will pursue the matter until some radical alteration is effected."

The only comment I have to make on that article is that it is only too true. As also is this, which deals with the question of working during meal hours. It is from the *Factory Times* of February 11th, 1896:

"In our last week's issue a Bolton spinner drew attention to the number of mill accidents in the Oldham district, and said he took it that a large portion of the accidents were due to cleaning machinery whilst in motion, and that such a circumstance was clear evidence that the time has arrived when cleaning time should be enforced upon the members. Upon inquiry, we found that very few of the accidents referred to arose from cleaning machinery. Therefore, our correspondent was wrong in his conclusions. Nevertheless, we agree with him that it is high time meal hour working should be abolished in all cotton mills, and that proper time should be allowed for the cleaning and oiling of the machinery during the ordinary working hours. The present system of working against each other is productive of more harm than the mill hands are aware of, and it is fast leading up to the driving system, which will become unbearable by the strongest of workers, let alone those who are inclined to be physically weak. There is much truth in what 'Young Minder' says, when he says that cotton operatives work twelve hours per day in place of ten, and in the end are not one penny better off. He hits the point in saying that the operatives ought to start with the engine and stop when it stops. It is a disgrace to the industry that there should be so much working in meal hours; and as the operatives are the proper parties to put a stop to the practice, the blame rests with them, and not with their employers, managers, and overlookers. So long as the workers rest, and are content to be driven like dumb animals, so sure are the mill officials likely to take advantage of their weakness, and make them work all the hours they possibly could. In fact, we have good proof of this in the manner in which managers and overlookers tell the spinners that they must piece their straps and bands, and do their cleaning and oiling in the meal times, and must not stop their mules for anything during engine hours except to doff the cops. In this way spinners are pushed to follow a practice which is a curse upon factory life, as with the quick speeds and often inferior material, the lot of spinners and piecers is very hard to bear from early morning till night. The only way of reducing the strain, both upon body and mind, is to enjoy the full benefit of the meal hours which Parliament in its wisdom provided for them. If the cotton operatives will not avail themselves of their rights in this way, we shall have to give them up as being almost past the limits of being educated in matters relating to their welfare as wage earners."

And here is a letter, taken from the correspondence column of the *Factory Times* dated February 14th, 1896, on the same subject:

"The race during the last ten years has been increasing pace by pace from a workman's point of view, and where we shall land one can scarcely prophesy. A large number of men are now claiming infirm benefit at the ages between forty-two and fifty. Increased speed, stricter attention to work, causing more anxiety and a greater strain upon nerve and strength, mean that something must be done to combat with the existing state of things which make men old long before their really appointed time. Is it a fact, in the province to which the speaker referred, that men go in at 5.30 A.M. in the morning and don't come out till 5.30 in the evening, working breakfast time and dinner time, and getting their meals when they can, or, if they don't stop in to their meals, they are hurry-scurrying back and don't give their food a chance of doing them any good? In the Bolton district it is now a pleasure to see men (minders) and lads (piecers) going to their dinners, and having a comfortable chat on the way and at the mill gates when they get back. Surely they must be better able to combat with their work after the rest and change, than if they were in the dens twelve hours at one spell without change of air or proper rest. I cannot understand cotton operatives clamouring for something which they haven't got, when they have not the wisdom to use the liberties which they have got, when they work twelve hours per day instead of ten, and in the end are not one penny better off. Meal hour work gives an opportunity for the unscrupulous and the avaricious to strive against their fellows, compelling them to do the same, or otherwise seek fresh pastures. Talking is very good sometimes, but actions speak louder than words, and to stop the unscrupulous the opportunity must be done away with, and let every man start off the proper mark, to work with the engine, and stop when it stops. There is another point for consideration. Why does the amalgamation not adopt some scheme of superannuation for those members who get old and get turned off? They cannot get labouring like they once could, as young men are too plentiful at the present day. It is very sad to see men getting a bit of a job here and there, and feeling very unhappy in having to be dependent upon other people, instead of spending the latter portion of their life contented, with a nice little income to keep them from the workhouse, or, as they very often term it, 'of feeling in the way.' If Bolton and Oldham would pull together they would be able to gain their rights; but if they are too blind to see their interest they will lose their power and might.—Yours truly, YOUNG MINDER."

That letter, also, is true in every detail.

I am pleased to say that the physical deformities so noticeable in factory operatives twenty or thirty years ago are not so plentiful to-day. The "factory leg," or bow-leg, once so common amongst the male operatives (and probably caused by the spinners, when young piecers, carrying the heavy skips down to the warehouse, which work is now done by a hoist), is not so frequently met with. But the general height of the Lancashire people has decreased much this last half-century. The Lancashire men of to-day are not as big as their grandfathers. This fact is corroborated by the gradual lowering of the height for recruits joining the army; it has been lowered an inch or two this last twenty years.[1]

I cannot prove whether this next matter has anything much to do with the factory system, but lunacy is greatly on the increase in Lancashire, the present asylum accommodation being inadequate; but no doubt the factory system, by the increased work and worry, contributes a good share of the imbeciles to the asylums. It is well known that monotony is a cause of insanity, and there is nothing more drearily monotonous than factory work. Suicides are numerous amongst factory operatives, too; the cases of young girls driven to take their own lives by the bullying of overseers, or the hard work (or both combined), are sadly too numerous. There are no statistics on this point; but I can recall five or six instances in

[1] Indeed, the height of the inhabitants seems decreasing all over the country. In 1875, out of every 1000 men in the British army, 285 were between 5ft. 7in. and 5ft. 8in.; in 1880, the 285 had gone down to 209; in 1885, to 198; in 1890, to 184; while during the same years the soldiers under 5ft. 5in. had increased from 65 to 115 per thousand.— Barker's " Facts and Figures."

Bolton and district this last two or three years.[1]
Also, in the *Annual Report* (for 1897) of the
Royal Albert Asylum, Lancaster, I find that the
greatest number of imbeciles come from the manufacturing towns, as thus : Manchester and Salford
77, Oldham 20, Bolton 12, Rochdale 9 ; but there
is no evidence to prove that these are cotton
operatives.   The *Bolton Journal* for May 7th, 1898,
says there is " considerable increase in the number
of lunatics in Bolton district of late years," and,
after mentioning the proposal for a new asylum for
the neighbourhood, says all the Lancashire asylums
are crowded, there being in the various county
asylums 570 imbeciles from Bolton.

[1] Taking up the evening paper after finishing this article
I find an account of a weaver girl's suicide on account of bad
work, at Leyland (17th December 1897).   Scarcely a week
goes by without a similar suicide in Lancashire or Yorkshire.

DANGERS OF THE FACTORY SYSTEM

Chapter I

ACCIDENTS, AND ILL-USAGE OF CHILDREN

Now to show that the factory system, in spite of all legislation, is yet dangerous and deadly.

I take, at random, the *Factory Times*, the organ of the textile operatives, for November 15th, 1895. (I may here repeat that this book was begun in 1895.) In this one weekly issue I find the following eight factory accidents: Young woman at Oldham, scalp wound, had to be taken to the Infirmary; young man taken to Oldham Infirmary with both arms broken and one thigh dislocated; a minder (adult), fractured arm, and badly lacerated, at Waterhead; a little piecer (boy) injured, at Waterhead; a spinner, at Preston, both thighs broken; a suicide, at Stalybridge, through trade depression; engine tenter injured, at Higham; man killed in a Macclesfield mill.

Accidents in the mill occur almost daily, and there are numbers of small accidents that never get reported in the papers. It will be noticed that I have included a suicide through trade depression.

Suicides from this cause are very numerous in the textile trades, as well as from other fears connected with employment. In a previous number of the *Factory Times* I find the case of a man who shot himself, because he dreaded that the introduction of certain labour-saving machinery would cast him out of work. Then another man poisoned himself because he was discharged after *thirty-five years faithful service*—probably because he was getting too old to work.

Here are more accident figures, from the Board of Trade returns for October 1895. In factory and workshop during this October 49 persons were killed; there were 174 amputations, 65 fractures, 4 loss of eye or eyes, 71 persons injured on head or face, and 654 other injuries—making in all 959 injured and 49 killed in a month's time, or at the rate of 10,000 injured per year, and 588 killed per year. Add to these figures 89 killed and 731 injured in mines, and 45 workers killed and 566 injured on railways—much of which labour would not be necessary but for the cotton trade—and we get an appalling total of victims annually slain in the interests of trade and commerce. Even as I am writing this, I read in the paper the case of a Bradford firm being fined £40 for having an unguarded loom, the shuttle of which flew out and blinded in one eye a young woman of twenty-six.[1]

It may be alleged that things are not the same now as in 1895; that I have purposely picked out

[1] *Northern Daily Telegraph*, November 23rd, 1895.

a certain week of accidents to support my conten-
tions. Let us see, then. While I am revising,[1] I take
the current issue of the *Factory Times* (November
19th, 1897) and find: Accident to male cardroom
operative, at Shaw ; two male factory hands, taken
to Oldham Infirmary, with broken legs; leg
amputated, at Stockport; girl aged sixteen, at
Skipton, caught in machinery, shockingly muti-
lated, and killed ; young man, at Rochdale, badly
hurt ; girl's hand taken off, at Wigan ; woman, at
Dudley Hill, caught in machinery, through being
pushed by the overseer,—eight accidents in all.
And in this issue of the *Factory Times* one of the
local correspondents says, " the number of accidents
is greatly on the increase." Which needs no
comment from me.

Take any issue of the *Factory Times*, past,
present, or immediate future, and you will find the
same awful tale of accidents weekly.

As I have quoted the Board of Trade accident
returns for 1895, I will also give the report issued
while I am revising this chapter. The following
figures are from the *Labour Gazette*, November
1897 : In factories and workshops, 47 killed, and
3499 injured, an increase of over 2000 in the
"injured " as compared with the same month for
1895. These tragic figures vary little whichever
month of the year you take.

From accidents we will turn to the rough usage

[1] For newspaper publication. These chapters were first
published in the *Clarion*.

of children in the factories. Most overseers are bullies, many are mere slave-drivers; and there are many instances on record of young girls being driven to suicide solely by brutal overseers. I well remember three cases I have known myself this last two years. Yet the law is powerless to prevent these murders, for such they are. Imagine what the pain and torture must be to drive a young girl to suicide; and then think how many bear the agony rather than end it in self-destruction. In the *Factory Times* (Yorkshire edition) I find several cases of children ill-treated by overseers. One dragged a girl by the hair of her head from one end of the room to the other; another beat a boy severely about the head, and kicked him. Not one-tenth of the cases of this sort, however, get into the papers. The children are generally too frightened to complain to their parents, lest they should get "sacked," or be further punished by the spite of the overseer. Of course, there are overseers who are kind and humane, but they are not plentiful. Moreover, because of the system and its slave-driving tendencies, even the overseer who is inclined to gentleness must be harshly domineering, in order to keep his situation, and force the workpeople to the pace of the machinery.

Chapter II

EFFECTS ON MIND

LET us now see how the factory system is bad for the mind and morals. One cannot give figures to prove this effect, but anyone who has mixed much amongst factory folk will soon discover that their mental strength is not great. They cannot bear any long strain of thought or study; they prefer light and sensational reading. For poetry and good literature they have no inclination. Their minds, like their bodies, are weakened, and crave spiced and seasoned rubbish, even as at every mouth-meal their sickly appetites must be coaxed with pickles, vinegar, or some other saliva stimulant.

Indeed, the factory operatives when their day's work is done are too weary and "fagged out" to engage in mental pursuits; they want something exciting, to take with variety the eye that is tired of monotony, to rouse the jaded body, and so they plunge into the noisy pleasures of stimulants and singing-rooms. Some few seek recreation in Sunday-school work and prayer-meetings, but these are the minority; the majority want stirring amusement, lively and intoxicating — something to make them forget. A visit to the homes of factory folk will prove what I say; not in one house in fifty will you find a bookshelf; not one man in a hundred will you find who has any first-hand knowledge of the great authors of his country's literature. Factory folks read the newspapers, of course; but it bears out my contention when I state the fact that they invariably turn to the murders, divorces, wars, etc., first, and will even read the advertisements before the editorial leaders, or book notices.

It would seem that machinery tends to make machines of those who work it; reducing the brain to a sort of stupidity, to a level with the mechanism it manipulates; making men very much lower than the angels, and a little higher than machines, with sufficient power of thought for automatic factory work, but a paralysation of all other mental functions, and incapability of close and original thinking. This fact, as I have said before, explains the inability of factory operatives to take up any prolonged mental study. They have literally become mere "hands." To use a botanical term, the head is "suppressed," or at least dormant; there being no use for it (in the factory scheme) it dies out as evolution teaches us that certain animal limbs and vegetable organs wither and eventually disappear when the creature's (or plant's) mode of life no longer needs them. It may happen, if the factory system continues, that the operatives' heads will, in course of time, shrink to a rudimentary fraction of empty skull, just as man to-day has at the base of his spinal column the bit of bone which proves that he once sported a simian tail.

A friend of mine, for ten years a factory operative, sends me the following as his opinion of the factory system: "Fifty years ago the factory operative described his condition by the phrase 'Tied to a bell.' To-day his position is narrowed still further. The bell has almost disappeared, for the simple reason that competition for places amongst the operatives themselves makes tolling unnecessary, while the engine, to which the bell was town-crier, remains. The factory hand is a machine. Health, morals, religion, citizenship, are no part of the factory system, except so far as they are thrust upon it by influences naturally foreign to it. . . . In other machine-using occupations the various parts of the whole process are less rigid in their connection. In the cotton mill you have the power concentrated in the engine, to whose iron pulsations, throbbing through a stifling atmosphere, a large body of operatives twist and turn like marionettes round a steam organ. A healthy population never was reared under such conditions and never will be. The fact that mechanical improvements depreciate the brain value of the operative makes the matter worse. I should advise all exploiters of labour to study some scheme of vaccination by which the worker can be evoluted or devoluted into exact accord with his machine, until they fit like bolt and nut. The weaver could then weave like a loom, the spinner spin like a 'mule,' while others could slub like a slubber, reel like a reel, cop like a cop, and bob like a bobbin."

This friend thus summarises the evils of the factory system to-day: " Cleaning in mill hours, no time for either mastication or needed rest; maternity and mill work; half-timers and recreation; cleaning dangerous machinery in motion; 'bating' (that is fining) and victimising; competition among piece-workers; blind windows; heat, dust, and floss (cotton fluff and dust); vapour of steam and oil fumes; bad sanitary conveniences." He also says, " We want more of the quality of the detective and less of the policeman in our factory inspectors; courage in operatives to enforce laws enacted for their special benefit, with an ambition to improve the condition of their neighbour 'next wheels,' instead of every man Jack bending his energies to best his mate, on the off chance of becoming a boss."

Another young man, a factory operative for ten years, says: " I noted that my fellow-workers were flat-chested, often suffered from headache and indigestion, and had weak lungs and sallow faces. . . . I have known some of them drill small holes in the window-sills, to which they would put their mouths for a waft of fresh air. But the overlookers plugged these holes up. . . . The factory operative loses all energy of body and mind—especially the latter."

This young man worked in the spinning-room till the age of twenty-one. His face was white, his body lean, he always looked ill.   By rare good luck he managed to get into journalism in a rural district.   Since then the healthful change in him is wonderful.   Ruddy face, strong limbs, and freedom from the headaches that formerly oppressed him severely.   I here give his account of factory life in his own words :

"My workmates were all victims to some ailment or other.   We started work at 6 o'clock in the morning—sometimes before—and were allowed half-an-hour for breakfast, 8 o'clock to 8.30.   But owing to the necessity of having to clean the machinery we did not get more than fifteen minutes for this meal.   I have sometimes been obliged to dispose of breakfast, consisting of bread, ham and eggs, or cheese, and a pint of hot tea or coffee, in five minutes, and this in a room with a temperature from 80 to 100 degrees.

"Owing also to the necessity of cleaning machinery we seldom had more than half-an-hour for dinner, including the time of going and returning home.   This hurried manner of taking meals, with the stifling heat of the rooms, the stench arising from the steam pipes, the unpleasant odour from oil and grease, the rumbling of shafts and drums, and the squeaking of smaller wheels and spindles made us sick and languid.   We never knew what it was to have a robust appetite.   One man would sometimes consume a quart of cold water per day, which generally produced a very bad effect on his physical system.   Speaking for myself, I was called at 5 o'clock each morning, with the most disgusting feelings in my head and stomach — nearly always inclined to vomit, my body being in a feverish condition. Naturally, like most of my mates, I was usually pale and dyspeptic.

" My wages were sufficient to keep me well housed and well clothed, but my want of health prevented me being at all contented with my position. Sometimes, I remember, an operative would have given anything for a breath of fresh air, the air in the spinning room having become so foul that the respiratory organs could only act with great difficulty. Under such circumstances, my fellow-workers always reminded me of a herd of beasts, confined to the limits of a narrow cage, and panting for forests, hills, and open plains. It was common to see some operatives with medicine bottles hidden in their pockets whilst at the mill. Many of them frequented quack doctors, who flourish in manufacturing towns.

" The labour is monotonous. The wages, and the inability to secure outside employment, are about the only inducements that keep the workers to their weary round. It seldom takes a mill-hand long to lose nearly all his elasticity and energy of body and mind—especially the latter, and, as a whole, they are a very uninteresting class of people. The spinners, too, spinning the same counts, are always expected to produce an equal quantity of yarn each week. To come below a fellow-worker in this respect jeopardises one's position.   Much discontent arises from this source, as each worker is compelled to toil on from morning to night, and from day to day, weak or strong, ill or well, in order to keep apace with the iron wheels and spindles, until he becomes like a mere piece of the machinery himself."

One comment I may make on the preceding. From our friend's breakfast bill of fare one might suppose the factory piecers fare luxuriously. Our friend's is an exceptional case ; he had a good home ; his parents were in good circumstances, keeping a provision shop. There are many piecers who get little besides bread and butter and tea for breakfast. There are many others, men between ages of twenty-one and thirty, who are married and bringing up families on their 13s. or 14s. per week. Of course, in these cases, the wife has to work too.

I might as well state here that piecers are employed directly by the operative spinner, who has full control over them, and is really, in their case, a middleman betwixt employer and piecer. It looks as if the operative spinners, though big trade unionists themselves, sweat their employés, the piecers, as much as possible.

Finally, there is my own case ; I was troubled with chest complaints in the factory town, but have got entirely rid of these ailments since I came to live in a place where the air is clear and pure. There is also the case of my own brothers and sisters who work in the mills; they are always more or less ill, and I don't suppose they are weaker physically than the majority of folks. Very strong healthy people are not much affected by factory work perhaps, at least, not for years. But these are rare. There are few really strong and healthy people amongst the working-manufacturing classes.

In 1856 the cotton imported to England was 895,115,000 lbs., which was spun on 28,000,200 spindles, averaging $31\frac{3}{4}$ lbs. each spindle.[1] In 1896 the cotton imported was 1,754,890,256 lbs., which was spun on 40,511,934 spindles, averaging $43\frac{1}{3}$ lbs. per spindle.[2] The spindles now turn off much more in less hours. Further on we shall note the effect of this increased "speeding." At this point, however, it should be noticed that though the spindles have increased by 12,000,000 since 1856 the number of workers has only increased 117,000 since 1868,[3] pointing to the deduction that there is much less labour per spindle nowadays than formerly. Other figures prove this inference.[4] In 1837 the labour per 1000 spindles was 7 operatives; in 1887 the labour per 1000 spindles was 3 operatives. That is in England. On the Continent the labour per 1000

[1] French's "Life of Samuel Crompton."

[2] Statistical Abstract for 1896.

[3] Plener's "Factory Legislation."

[4] "The Cotton Trade in England and on the Continent," by Schultze Gævernitz.

spindles is double, and in some cases more than
double that in England.   In Switzerland there
are 6 operatives to 1000 spindles, in Bavaria the
same, in Saxony 7 operatives per 1000 spindles,
and in Russia 16,[1] which tends to show that the
Englishman can be driven to do much more work
than the foreigner.   The "foreign competition"
boot is all on the other leg, at least so far as the
cotton trade is concerned.

Gævernitz [2] says that the factory system "has
produced a new type of industrial worker . . .
born and educated for the machine.   It is not
bodily power which distinguishes him, . . . but
with increasing size and speedy machines, with
augmenting productive power and complication,
a continually increasing brain power is demanded
from the operative."   But, as I have said, and,
I think, proved by other evidence and that of
witnesses, the contrary is the case.   If the factory
operatives thought much they would—well, make
an alteration in the present social system.   Have
not reformers of all kinds always found the factory
population slow to understand and accept any
schemes of betterment?

Why?   Not because those factory folks would
not be glad to have easier conditions of life, but
because their minds have become so indifferent
from torpidity that they cannot make an effort to

[1] " The Cotton Trade in England and on the Continent,"
by Schultze Gævernitz.
[2] The same.

grasp and reason out of theory into practice the possibilities of amelioration and reform. True, candidates for Parliament always address the factory electorate as "intelligent working-men," "hard-headed toilers," etc., but is not that of itself ample proof of the contrary?

The factory operative rarely goes in for study of science, or philosophy, or anything; he cannot stand the strain of close thought. He sometimes spurs himself to a course of technical study, but —that is always with a view to improving his material position by qualifying for an overseer or manager.

Speaking on the Ten Hours Bill, years ago, Lord Macaulay said: "If ever we (Britain) are compelled to retire from the paramount position among the trading nations, we shall not give way to a race of degenerate dwarfs, but to some strong nation excelling us in physique and genius." This is likely to happen, though not exactly as Macaulay thought. We ourselves are becoming the degenerate dwarfs.

We are told that in ancient Rome—for Rome had a factory system—a mark or stigma was impressed upon all the operatives, so that none could quit the business or run away without detection. And if we look at the factory workers to-day, we shall find that they are branded as conspicuously as were the old Roman slaves. An observing man can tell the factory face anywhere.

F

SECTION V

FEMALE FACTORY WORKERS

Chapter I

FACTORY MORALITY

WE have seen the effects of the factory system on body and mind; let us now consider how it affects morality and female workers. The female factory workers of to-day are mostly weavers and cardroom hands. Formerly, females used to work with the male spinners, but the men's trade union has in most places put a stop to female employment in the spinning-room, though there is one mill at the present time, situated at Lostock, near Bolton, where there are still women spinners. The Bolton operative spinners, however, refuse to have the women in their union, or even to admit the men who work for the same firm. Practically, to-day, the male operatives have a monopoly of the mule-spinning, but in weaving, the women have almost entirely superseded the men, except on heavy looms. The machinery that ousted the hand-loom weaver, has also ousted the men; one female can nowadays manage four looms with the assistance of a girl.

Factory morality has improved since the days when men and women worked together half-naked, the females with short skirts and bare legs, and, from the nature of their duties, frequently making compulsory indecent exposures of their person as they reached over the mule-carriage to "piece up." Some operative spinners (as bad as their masters) used to make seduction one of the conditions under which they engaged a young woman. But matters are bad enough still, as how can they help but be in a state of society where managers and overseers have almost life-and-death power over female employés?

One cannot give statistics to demonstrate this evil, but a few instances will suffice. There is alive to-day (or was not long ago), not far from Manchester, an employer who makes seduction one of the conditions on which females may have work at his establishment. If they decline, they must quit. Single or married makes no difference, and the same rule applies to the girl of sixteen, and the woman of thirty. How many victims have fallen to this gentleman it would be difficult to estimate, but he has been enforcing this game for many, many years. There are many employers like him; I knew two or three myself some years ago.

Last year, in the *Factory Times*, there was an account of a woman who was discharged because she refused to be seduced by the mill manager. Not that the villain was fool enough to give that as a reason for the dismissal; some trifling fault, easily found or made in a factory, with the woman's work, was the reason given for the discharge. For one case of this sort that gets into print, there are dozens never heard of beyond the locality in which they occur.

The loose sanitary arrangements of most mills produce loose conduct. The conveniences are often in a place exposed to the gaze of all the operatives. I know a modern mill where the male operatives have to pass through the female workers to the closets, which lie right alongside the machines on which the women work.

Dr Gould, medical officer for Bolton, in his report for 1897, says: "According to the Factory Acts, 'sufficient and suitable' conveniences have to be provided, the interpretation of 'suitable' being left to the Sanitary Authority. On our register (Bolton) we have at present, excluding bakehouses, 163 factories, and 586 workshops. I am not yet prepared to say in how many of the factories the sanitary conveniences are not 'sufficient and suitable,' but as to other defects, the following have been found—65 cesspools, and 24 without fire-escapes."

There is, in consequence, much indecent talk in the factories and weaving-sheds, as well as many a rude improvisation, for vulgar diversion, of Phallic ceremonies, articles used in the workroom being employed for illustrative purposes. Yet, on the whole, I do not think the factory operatives, especially the females, are so loose in conduct as loose in talk; though there is a good deal of sexual intercourse between young persons, not promiscuous, but between courting couples, before marriage. And my opinion is that this suggestive talk and stirring of animal instincts is caused by men working as overseers amongst the women, whose employment necessitates short skirts, scanty clothing, and consequently a greater or less display of those portions of the female form which excite the sex-passion in the male.

Possibly, too, the hot atmosphere of the factories forces maturity sooner into the bodies mentally and physically weakened by mill life; and this fact is also responsible for factory foulness of mouth and morals. Engels, in his book, "The Condition of the Working Classes in England in 1844," expresses the same view. He writes: "An estimate of sexual morality cannot readily be reduced to figures, but if I may trust my own observations and the general opinion of those with whom I have spoken, as well as the tenor of the testimony furnished me, the aspect of the influence of factory life upon the morality of the youthful female is most depressing. . . . The employment of young girls produces all sorts of irregularities during the period of development. In some the heat of the factories hastens this process, so that in some cases girls of thirteen and fourteen are wholly mature. Robertson relates in the *North of England Medical and Surgical Journal* that he had seen a girl of eleven years, who was not only a wholly developed woman, but pregnant, and that it was by no means rare in Manchester for women (?) to be confined at fifteen years of age. In such cases the influence of the warmth of the factories is the same as that of a tropical climate ; and, as in such climates, the abnormally early development revenges itself by correspondingly premature age and debility. On the other hand, retarded development of the female constitution occurs, and the breasts mature late or not at all."

My own observation and experience—and that of male and female friends working in the factories —corroborate the foregoing even to-day. I knew the parties in a recent case in Bolton, where a mill girl of fifteen had a child ; and—if the lad's talk to his companions is to be relied upon—by her brother. This girl would not divulge the paternity. The girl was physically a fully-developed woman. There is no necessity to detail other instances ; they are frequent in all the great cotton towns.

Chapter II

THE EFFECTS ON CHILD-BEARING WOMEN

As Engels says, in other words, the female factory operatives are old women at thirty. It is painfully astonishing to note the rapid ageing in factory females after the age of twenty. They seem to collapse, in one shrinking, wrinkling fall, from girls to old women, especially after marrying and having the first child. The first pregnancy seems to break them up altogether, and they never, as they ought to do in a natural healthy state, regain their pre-marital bloom, which it is evident must be at best only a canker-bloom, destroyed by the first maternal strain on the system. I have seen many factory girls, of twenty-five years of age to thirty, whose heads were swiftly going grey ; I have known several who were quite grey, and looked sixty years old at the age of thirty. It is needless to state that all these deteriorations must tell on the offspring of such females, even to the third and fourth generation. And when to a factory mother is added a factory father—what worth the children then ?

When female factory operatives marry, they usually continue at work till within a day or two of the birth of the first child. Many of them used to get back to work again as soon as they could after the confinement ; in many cases less than a week after. This they did mostly for fear of losing their places. But now the law prevents them. The Factory Act of 1891 (came in force January 1st, 1893) prohibits the employment of women within four weeks after confinement.

But, which is far more important, there is no prohibition as to pregnancy. The woman can only principally injure herself by working after confinement ; by working before, she injures the unborn child. A female weaver has very heavy weights to lift and adjust several times a day, and this strain must be hurtful to both mother and embryo. Pregnant women should certainly not be in the factory at all. I must admit, however, that many married women like the mill. This age of competition makes them grabbingly selfish in the struggle for existence. Further, some women prefer the crowded factory to the quiet home, because they have a hatred of the solitary housework. I have often heard married females say that they would rather be in the factory than in the house, because the comparative isolation gave them the dumps after being used to the company of hundreds of workmates.

I am afraid, too, that the female factory operatives themselves would offer great resistance to any law proposing to restrict pregnant women. The legal editor of the *Factory Times* agrees with me on this point. He says : " The Factory Acts do not apply to a woman who is pregnant ; they only affect her so far as regards four weeks after confinement, during which time her employment is prohibited. When a woman is in such a condition, it rests with herself whether she works or not, as an employer cannot necessarily be expected to know that she is going to have a child ; and if any further factory legislation was introduced dealing with the matter, it would mean a loss of work which the women hands would be likely to resent."

Truly this is a sad state of things for a Christian

and civilised nation; that a woman should be obliged to consider everything else before her highest and holiest duty—maternity. We are more humane with our cattle than with our women.

Instances of children actually born in weaving-sheds are numerous. There was a report of one in the *Factory Times* not long ago; the woman was delivered in the midst of thundering looms, in a shed full of other operatives, male and female, young and old. The child died while itself and mother were being taken in a cab to the hospital.

It is horrible to think how many children are blighted and blasted even before they are born by suffering gestation under such conditions; at a period when, for the sake of the life that she carries within her, a woman ought to dwell in the kindliest and sweetest surroundings, under best hygienic influences, kept healthy by easy exercise in fresh air, and not fagged and en-feebled by grinding hard labour in a foul, steamy, hot atmosphere. Engels states the case of a factory woman in the last stage of pregnancy who was fined sixpence for sitting down. That was fifty years ago. To-day she dare not—she can-not—sit down. The relentless machinery will not let her.

For all this folly, for all this cruel treatment of women caused by the present factory system, the innocent children (as usual!) have to pay—

have to pay in lives that are not lives, but merely suffering existences that were better ended and best never begun.

Mention must be made of the compulsory side of the question. Many married women are compelled to work in the factory because the husband's wage is not sufficient to keep the house going; though there are also many women, in comparatively good circumstances, who work out of sheer greed, or in order to spend their earnings in fine feathers for themselves. These latter (to look at the case another way) keep many a starving sister out of employment.

Often factory mothers (who are at work during the child-suckling period) endure great pain from breasts full of milk that runs from them in waste instead of feeding those for whom Nature produced it. Yet these women cannot leave their toil to go home and feed their babies; these latter are being brought up on "the bottle" by some neighbour; and all medical men agree that the "feeding-bottle" is but a poor substitute for mothers' milk. Not content with sweating the fathers and mothers, the factory system must needs rob the babies of their natural dues; nay, must, as has been shown, actually begin to injure them before they are born.

My wife's mother tells me that when she was a weaver the milk from her breasts has run till she has been wet through, and she has been in such pain that her husband, who worked in the same shed, has, at the risk of being detected and reprimanded, or losing his place, left his work to fetch the children to the mother's relief. Why did she not stay at home? Well, she was forced to work with her husband to keep the family in food.

And I know the case of my own mother. She was a "winder," and I was born during the "cotton panic," when my father was out of work, and my mother was compelled to become the bread-winner. I was nursed by my grandmother while my mother toiled at a factory a couple of miles distant from our dwelling. During the dinner-hour—sixty minutes nominally, often only forty or forty-five really—my mother would run home in order to suckle me, get her own meal, and be back at the mill before work restarted. What sort of milk, poisoned by the worry and hurry, must that have been for me?

SECTION VI

EFFECTS OF THE FACTORY SYSTEM ON CHILDREN

Chapter I

HALF-TIMERS

WE have seen how factory employment generally affects females; how it unfits them for good motherhood, and has an injurious effect upon family life, when the mother works in the mill instead of attending to her children herself. There are also many minor evils attendant upon female factory life—loss of sleep, loss of rest, whimsical appetites, indigestion, anæmia, shrinkage of stature, bent backs (most weavers, as I have stated before, eventually develop a disfiguring stoop), ignorance of cooking (which acts disastrously on the husband), deficiency in domestic qualifications (through being all day at the mill), and many other lesser evils; but as it would take a book to detail fully all these things, we will leave them at the bare statement, and proceed to a consideration of the effects of the factory system on children. And this is the saddest chapter of all.

According to the Statistical Abstract for 1894 there are 48,133 half-time boys and girls (25,432 being girls) in the cotton trade; in the woollen trade 4934; in the worsted trade 18,000; a total of 101,000 half-timers in cotton, woollen, and worsted factories alone.

Here, again, figures give but small idea of the hideous truth. One cannot put pale faces, thin health, weary heads, into statistics very well. The children, as in most other human affairs, have always suffered most under the factory system. They are the youngest, the weakest, subject to their parents as well as to their environment; and it is often difficult to determine which is harsher on the children, their parents or their country.

When I read the accounts of the factory cruelties at the beginning of this century I rage between roaring wrath and tears of pity; I feel ashamed of my countrymen, of my county; I cry, that the Lancashire people were never fit to be parents; I say, that the factory system was a system of torture and murder, as dreadful as any massacres of Christians by Turks; a disgrace in the story of any race or age; a big, ghastly, horrible stain of blood on the history of England. As I write, pictures of the past rise before me; pictures for the present to weep over, and for the future to shudder at. I see the little innocents rudely dragged from bed to be pitched into the factories at the early age of three and four; I see them stunted, sickly, with sad eyes imploring

mercy from parents and masters in vain; I see
them pining, failing, falling, struggling against
hell and death, knowing not what to do for relief,
knowing not where to ask for aid, dying by
agonising inches, and blest when the end comes;
wondering dully, no doubt, in their day-long
torture and night-long feverishness, what they are,
and where they are, and how they came to this
fate, and what these tormentors called fathers
and mothers and overseers brought them here
for, and what they ultimately mean to do with
them; and thus they exist—alive, but breathing
and eating slow death, sleeping in death, with
no flowers, nor grass, nor toys, nor any childish
joy in their young lives; not knowing, and therefore unable to take any pride in the fact, that
they are being crushed into the mortar wherewith
to build the commercial glory of England, that
shall rise to such admirable splendour over their
dust; not thinking that there must be sacrifice
and victims, as in all noble causes, and thus they,
being unable to help themselves, might as well
be slaughtered as any other, so that in years to
come a rich manufacturing aristocracy may rule
and govern the debilitated offspring of such of
them as survive to breed more slaves; while
pampered historians, writing on gilt-edged paper,
in villas built out of this brutality, shall point
to the factory system as the triumph of the
nineteenth century, the source—of course, along
with the Bible (that so strongly denounces the

ill-treatment of "these little ones")—of England's dominion over land and sea, and the happy model of individualist-centralised industry for all nations to the end of the world. That is one scene I see, "the most frightful picture of avarice, selfishness, and cruelty on the part of masters and of parents, and of juvenile and infantine misery, degradation, and destruction, ever presented."[1]

There are succeeding pictures, all as horrible, but here we have not space for them—pictures of factories and coal-pits,—out of which has come the commercial glory of which England is so proud to-day; the world-streaming banner, that is (to those who have eyes to see) funeral-banded with black smoke and splotched with great rusty spots of dried blood. "One-fourth of the children (in the early days of the factory system) were crippled or otherwise deformed."[2] Their history is "simply appalling, and would be incredible were it not fully borne out by evidence from other sources."[3]

Such, in brief, were the earliest effects of the factory system on children. Matters have certainly improved since those days; the factory system is not so hard upon the children now.

[1] Parliamentary Commission of 1840, and Mr Nassau Senior's address to the Social Science Congress, Edinburgh, 1862.

[2] "The Factory System," by R. Cooke-Taylor.

[3] The same.

But it is not good ; it never will be good.   The
half-timers of to-day may look fairly healthy when
they first enter the factory, but a couple of years
takes all the bloom out of them, and gives them
a singularly wizened and withered appearance,
transforming them from pleasant, plump fairies
into shrivelled, uncanny elves.   Plener says :
"The progress of these half-timers, singularly
enough, is not inferior to that of other children
who go to school twice a day, which may be
explained by the circumstance that their early
familiarity with work and consequent earning of
wages causes a speedier development of intelligence in the factory children."[1]

Plener is one-quarter right and three-quarters
wrong.   Half-timers are sometimes sharper than
other children for a few months ; then they
become drowsy and stupid.   The "early familiarity with work" certainly forces their intelligence
up ; but, like all forced maturity, it soon collapses ;
and the children's mentality quickly becomes of
the same character as that of the factory adults,
which I have previously described, and they are
unable to bring their minds to any real study.
They are quick, alert, at the beginning of their
factory life ; but this premature smartness soon
stupefies into the dull automatism common to
factory folk, who toil but think not.   I believe
that this lethargic mental condition accounts for
the apathy of the factory workers to their own

[1] "English Factory Legislation."

true interests; any reform that will benefit them is invariably begun and carried on by outsiders.

For eight years I taught in public elementary day schools in a cotton town, and in all the schools in which I was a teacher, there was a great proportion of half-timers; and I speak from experience when I say that I often pitied the half-timers and excused their lessons. I have seen them fall asleep over their lesson-books or tasks, after they have been in the factory all the morning (six hours). They were generally dull and sleepy, and it was often downright cruelty to force them along the curriculum fixed by the Education Code; but the schoolmaster, no matter how tender his heart, was forced to prick them to the pace, or risk censure, and perhaps loss of place, for not keeping his school up to the standard, and getting the expected amount of Government grant at the annual examination. In spite of the alleged sharpness of half-timers, no schoolmaster likes them. The testimony of all the teachers in Lancashire is with me on this point. The half-timers, as a rule, hamper and hinder the progress of the rest of the class.

Archdeacon Wilson of Rochdale, in an article on "Half-Timers," writes:—"There is the physical health point of view. Now, from this point it is perfectly clear that the children, especially from the neglected homes, suffer. I caused all the boys in my boys' school to be weighed and measured in the autumn of 1891, before the half-

G

time age was raised from ten to eleven. The results were disputed, and the Rochdale School Board of that date willingly took the matter up, and made similar measures in their schools. Their figures confirmed mine, and showed that while children who are not half-timers grow uniformly in height and weight from the age of eight to that of twelve, our Rochdale children, many of whom are half-timers, received a sudden check in the rate of growth at ten, and the lower rate was continued till the age of twelve. Our children are below the average size even at eight and nine, and ten, from many causes, chiefly improper food and early neglect; but the disparity was even greater at eleven and twelve. These measures were repeated at the end of 1894 in my school (the newly-elected School Board refused), and, since the half-time age had been raised in the meantime to eleven, the measures were of much interest. It became quite plain that the check in the growth at ten had disappeared, and that a much slighter check was apparent at eleven. In other words, these measures, so far as they went, proved that the work of these children in the mills from ten to eleven stunted their growth."[1]

The Lancashire cotton operatives, both spinners and weavers, are paid by "piece." They thus strive to turn off as much work as possible, and force the half-timers to keep the pace. The

[1] *Labour Leader*, 25th May 1895.

Factory Acts prohibit the cleaning of machinery
while in motion, but the half-timers are often
compelled by their masters to break the law;
for the greedy spinner does not like the wheels
to be stopped, not even for five minutes, because
his piece-work wage is thereby lessened a fraction.
It is plain, therefore, that numerous accidents
must happen; the half-timer loses a finger, or a
limb, and sometimes his life, while doing this
forbidden cleaning. [1]

"Sweeping under," while the machinery is in
motion, is a dangerous practice, though I did it
myself before the law was passed prohibiting it,
and once got caught, but luckily was only slightly
crushed, though another second's delay would
have meant my death. I must say, that I have
seen some nimble little piecers do this "sweeping
up" with a dexterous rush that compels admiration; but a moment's carelessness, a second's
miscalculation, means a frightful injury or bleed-
ing corpse. This "sweeping-under," consists in
sweeping, with a short brush, the space between
the advancing and receding mule-carriage and the
base-work creel. The mule-carriage slowly draws
out for two or three yards, then suddenly rushes
back like the shutting of a lid, and the piecer
has to slip out of the way in "half a jiffy," as

[1] I am pleased to state that the Bolton operative
spinners have insisted on having the engine stopped for
cleaning, and their courage and example are worthy
imitation.

he says. The loud click of the "faller" always warns him when the carriage is reversing.

As I have said, the accidents to children are appalling. For the quarter ending January 31st, 1890, 172 accidents were reported to the Bolton Operative Spinners' Association. This included accidents to adults; but they all arose from cleaning machinery while in motion.

The operative adult spinner's and big piecer's position, standing on the "wheel-head" to adjust a strap, is as dangerous as anything I know; while many a battle-field hero would shrink to do the cleaning of the "wheel-head," where all the fiercest wheels and snakiest straps are whirling and rushing,—a job that the spinner must tackle at least once a week.

"The last annual report of the Home Office gives a total of 627 accidents in the mills of Bolton and district, and 160 of these happened to little piecers from 'scroll bands' and 'carriage wheels' of self-acting mules."[1]

The law says that no women, nor young persons, shall be allowed to clean machinery in motion. But there are three hours cleaning each week for every worker employed on the spinning-mules, and the engine only stops one half-hour weekly, to allow this three hours' work to be done! No cleaning is done in the meal hours; it is not permitted (though this enactment is broken daily, by - the - by). There is therefore

[1] *Schoolmaster*, "Half-Timer Special," February 1895.

no course left but to do the cleaning while the engines are running, or—lose money. This the workers don't care to do. Wage is more valuable than the life or limb of man, woman, and child.

"In 1894 and 1897 the factory operatives of Lancashire and Yorkshire offered the most strenuous opposition to the raising of the half-time age to 12 years. Why was this? Because under the piece-work system the spinner or weaver is the employer of the child, and pays the half-timer out of his own earnings. Hence, the cheaper child labour is, the better pecuniarily for the spinner or the weaver."[1]

Money seems to be the first consideration with most cotton operatives; the health and happiness and even lives of their children, are but of very minor importance.

Here is proof of the preceding charge, which I am sorry to make, for it is not to the credit of Lancashire parents.

"I regret to say," says Mr Henderson, factory inspector, "that there are very frequent accidents arising from the violation of the Act, and I am afraid it is because of the instructions given to the children by the spinners."[2]

Further evidence from the Royal Commission on Labour testifies to the unhealthiness of factory work.

"The card-room operatives throughout Lanca-

[1] *Schoolmaster*, "Half-Timer Special," February 1895.
[2] Evidence before the late Royal Commission on Labour.

shire complain of the light, fibrous dust which is generated by the carding process. The ring and throstle spinners state that they suffer from the excessively high temperature of the spinning rooms, which in some mills reaches 100° F.

"I noticed several weavers whose lips were coated with white size-dust, and the medical officers of the districts attribute to this injurious material the various forms of lung disease from which weavers suffer who are employed upon heavily-sized warps."[1]

Then there is the "steaming" of weaving sheds; causing headaches and rheumatism.[2]

Dr Torrop, certifying surgeon, Heywood, says: "The promising child of ten degenerates into the lean and sallow young person of thirteen; and this process is continued until a whole population becomes stunted; and thus the conditions of life in factory towns become a real source of danger to England's future.

"After twenty-five years' observation of factory life, I have no doubt that the height, weight, and physique of Lancashire factory hands is below the average of England. The deficiency is greater in full-timers than in half-timers, and is not made up in adult life, but goes on in accelerated ratio. A specialised population of factory workers less muscular, but more highly strung, is being evolved."

[1] Evidence before the late Royal Commission on Labour.
[2] Royal Commission on Labour.

Again, Dr Torrop says: "It must be borne in mind that the medium average of Lancashire factory children is not equal to the average elsewhere. The latter standard is hardly reached by the 341 children described as superior (out of 2000 examined), *while the medium division (1106 of the 2000) is greatly below the standard of good health.* This is much more distinctly marked amongst children of 13, 'full-timers' who have passed some years in the factory, than it is in those of 10 years of age. Of 60 healthy children averaging 13½ years, and taken as they came (31 girls and 29 boys), the average weight was 74 lbs., or 14 lbs. below the average of good health elsewhere. The lower division of 324 (out of the 2000) included many defective and diseased cases, and, of course, the 78 residuum were poor indeed." [1]

"Strong children, though, survive the factory life; they go through it sturdily; but even they do not escape scot-free, for insidious diseases settle in their lungs, the blood is squeezed out of their faces, their limbs lose their youthful straightness and vigour. But delicate children have no chance at all, for that which only injures the healthy kills the frail quickly. Great home-lessons (for school), too, are thrust on half-timers, the reason for which is obvious. As the half-timer has only half a day at school, it is necessary to make him do a deal of work out of school, to

[1] *Schoolmaster,* "Half-Timer Special," February 1895.

prevent him falling behind in his learning; thus the poor half-timer is oppressed all round the circle. His labour in the mill, instead of being some claim for exemption from any other task during the day, becomes the cause of his being loaded with more than his due share of lessons. 'Unto him that hath shall be given; while he that is kicked by one shall feel the foot of all the crowd.'"

Now, on this subject of half-timers, here is something tragically ridiculous, proving what I have asserted about the stupefaction of the reasoning faculty in cotton operatives—especially the male portion. The Bolton Operative Spinners' Union, in their annual report, issued April 1891, enumerating the disadvantageous conditions under which the adult spinner has to labour, say: "He has to work in a temperature ranging from 80 to 110 degrees Fahrenheit, and in a vitiated atmosphere which is not completely changed even once a week. These conditions render him peculiarly liable to contracting chest complaints and rheumatic affections."

That is true, as medical evidence testifies. Now, read what the very same body of men, the Bolton Operative Spinners, said at a meeting held to consider the half-time question only a month after they had issued the report containing the preceding statement. Mark: "Having carefully considered the proposal to raise the age for half-timers from ten to twelve, we are strongly of opinion that such a step is entirely uncalled for, in the interest of the child itself, as, speaking with a full knowledge of the question, we do hereby assert that a child does not suffer, either physically or intellectually, as a result of becoming a half-timer, and we would, therefore, respectfully urge upon the Government not to accede to any demand for raising the age ! " [1]

That is not all. As if they had not already made themselves ridiculous enough, the same body of spinners a year later declared that "eight hours a day was sufficient for adults under such trying conditions ! " [2]

As the every-day journalist says, "comment would be superfluous ! "

But oh ! the tragedy of such a comedy !

And oh ! the children — the poor helpless children ! — condemned to be born of parents, and entrusted to the care of fathers who have less true affection for their offspring than a savage tiger.

I am reluctant to write it, but it is a sad fact, that the majority of parents in Lancashire regard children only as commercial speculations, to be turned into wage-earning machines as soon as the child's age and the law will permit. For this they oppose the raising of the age of half-timers ; for this resent all legislative interference, either educational or hygienic, in the matter of their children. Instead of fighting for wages to keep their children,

[1] May 1891.   [2] 1892.

they are cowardly enough to let the children be forced to keep them. If the children could only hold a congress and speak, what shameful revelations would be made! No wild beast ever treats its young as too many of the fathers and mothers of Lancashire have treated and still treat theirs. I write in all sorrow, for I am a Lancashire lad myself. A lion, a bear, even the basest of brutes, will fight to the death to protect their young; but a great many human beings in Lancashire—and elsewhere—are eager to turn their young to the most advantage by sacrificing them on the altar of trade for paltry pecuniary gain.

───────

Chapter II

HALF-TIME STATISTICS

I will close this disgraceful part of this account of the factory system of to-day by figures from a competent authority on half-timers, one who has made a special study of this subject—Mr Richard Waddington, schoolmaster, Bolton, an enthusiast who has for years fought alone and against fierce opposition in the righteous cause of the half-time children.

From facts and figures, and the *Schoolmaster*, "Half-Timer Special" (February 1895), sent me by Mr Waddington, I take the following :—

HALF-TIME SCHOLARS

From Returns of Schools Inspected for Year
ended 31st August 1892.

County.	Number of Half-time Scholars on the School Registers.
Bedfordshire	33
Berkshire	12
Buckinghamshire	256
Cambridgeshire	506
Cheshire	9,684
Cornwall	61
Cumberland	17
Derbyshire	2,912
Devonshire	278
Dorsetshire	210
Durham	...
Essex	146
Gloucestershire	216
Hampshire	66
Herefordshire.	...
Hertfordshire	298
Huntingdonshire	36
Kent (E. M.)	448
Lancashire	93,969 [1]
Leicestershire	4,577
Lincolnshire	443
Middlesex (E. M.)	79
Monmouthshire	3
Norfolk	90

[1] Half-time statistics of chief Lancashire towns.—Blackburn 7892, Oldham 6139, Bolton 5930, Preston 5836. (Leicester has 3271, Nottingham 1785.) It should be added that these figures include half-timers in all other trades besides cotton manufacture.

County.	Number of Half-time Scholars on the School Registers.
Northamptonshire	2,447
Northumberland	...
Nottinghamshire	2,283
Oxfordshire	...
Rutlandshire	2
Shropshire	88
Somersetshire	600
Staffordshire	4,652
Suffolk	119
Surrey (E. M.)	213
Sussex	81
Warwickshire	625
Westmorland	352
Wiltshire	287
Worcestershire	664
Yorkshire	44,791 [1]
London School Board District . .	693
Wales	126
England and Wales . . .	172,363

Compare Lancashire with all the other counties, to its shame !

———

Chapter III

ACCIDENTS TO CHILDREN, CHILD MORALITY, AND EFFECTS ON EDUCATION

As I mentioned in the section which dealt with mill accidents generally, the accidents to children

[1] Bradford (Yorks) 9286 (more than any single Lancashire town), Leeds 975.

are appalling. The Home Office Annual Report for 1894 gives a total of 160 mill accidents to children in Bolton and district—mostly from "scroll-bands" and "carriage wheels" of self-acting mules. Several lads who used to be schoolmates of mine are now without arm, leg, or hand, or have a finger or two missing. And many similar cases will be found in every cotton town. The law says that no women nor young persons shall be allowed to clean machinery in motion. But there are *three hours' cleaning* each week for every worker employed on the spinning-mules, and the *engine only stops half - an - hour* weekly to allow this three hours' work to be done. The result is, that the law is broken daily, and accidents are awfully numerous, for the spinner in charge of a mule will not stop the machine while cleaning is done, because he is paid by the piece, and every minute's stoppage means so much less wage. "I regret to say," says Mr Henderson, factory inspector, "that there are very frequent accidents arising from the violation of the Act, and I am afraid it is because of the instructions given to the children by the spinners." [1]

Evidence given before the Royal Commission on Labour proves the general unhealthiness of the factory system for children, and corroborates all the assertions I have made in the previous articles. And, quite recently, even as this book is going

[1] Evidence before the Royal Commission on Labour in 1895.

through the press (January 1899), the special commissioner of the London *Daily News*, in an investigating tour in the factory districts of Lancashire, emphatically points out the physical degeneration of the children. He says the little girls of twelve and thirteen looked more fit to be playing with dolls than working, while the half-time lads were three or four inches below the average height.[1]

Children's eyes are affected by the factory work too. "The sight of the children suffers very often from the fineness of the material. In a large school in the North of England, where the half-timer abounds, in the upper classes 200 scholars' eyes were tested. The result was 14 per cent. of the whole day scholars, 25 *per cent. of the half-timers*, failed to pass the prescribed test." All this evidence confirms my own experience at mill and school. But not half the shame and horror is told. There is the effect on morals.

Miss Abrahams, factory inspector, says: "Though the conditions of mill life in Lancashire are closely similar to those in Yorkshire, I found a larger number of cases of actual immorality and of immoral tendencies. I see no explanation for this except in the fact that the sanitary accommodation is much more frequently common to men and women in Lancashire than it is in Yorkshire. Two cases of immorality have

[1] London *Daily News*, first week in January 1899.
[2] *Schoolmaster*, "Half-Timer Special," February 1895.

been directly traced to this, and it is mentioned as the cause of much loose language and immoral behaviour. Moreover, common provisions for decency are sometimes absent, as in mill 375, where the lavatories, opening from the shed in which men and women work together, are unprovided with doors. In several cases, also, the sanitary accommodation for the women is situated in the taperoom, or in other rooms in which men only are employed."

Further, she reports : " I have made the most careful inquiry into the effect of mill life upon the morality of women, girls, and children, and I find that in a number of mills the overlookers do use loose and violent language, which it is considered has a harmful effect, *especially upon the children.* There are undoubtedly some few cases of direct immorality in connection with a system of 'favouritism' (*e.g.* No. 35), but a more general cause of immorality in girls and children is insufficient sanitary accommodation, the same closets being common in some mills to men, women, and children. Beyond this there is no special tendency to immorality among mill-workers."[1]

" The immorality of children is attributed, and probably correctly so, to the fact that the inadequate sanitary accommodation I have mentioned as being so injurious is most general

[1] Evidence of lady factory inspector, Miss Abrahams, before Royal Commission on Labour.

in spinning-rooms, and this is just the part of the mill where children are largely employed." [1]

Why prolong the harrowing tale? The effects on the children's schooling I have referred to before. Here is one more pathetic piece of evidence, showing that children themselves see and feel that the half-time system is not good: "Attended examination (Wednesday, 13th April) at one of the schools. The children seemed very eager to pass, and tried their best to answer the questions in geography, grammar, arithmetic, and so on, such as would certainly puzzle a large number of persons four times their age. The repeating of poetry was very good, but one poor little fellow, when asked by the inspector to recite his portion, rose up, but could not proceed. The other boys called out, 'Please, sir, he is a half-timer.' The little chap had not time to learn 'Shakespeare.' He had to work to help to keep himself. The three 'R's' would be as much as he would be able to learn." [2]

I found a very similar condition of things when I was a teacher; often the answers of the half-time children to examination questions were laughably ridiculous, and sometimes sadly humorous—sad

[1] Evidence of lady factory inspector, Miss Abrahams, before Royal Commission on Labour.

[2] From "Something Attempted, Something Done," a review of a year's work on the Bolton School Board, by Joseph Shufflebotham, a working-man member of that body, published Bolton 1892.

in the fact that they revealed the bitter home-life or hard work-life of the children. I give one instance to relieve the pitiful seriousness of these chapters. At the yearly examination of one school where I taught, the children (nine and ten years old) were questioned about Longfellow's "Village Blacksmith," that being one of the pieces of poetry they had learned in compliance with the Code. After one lad had recited the verse beginning, "Toiling, rejoicing, sorrowing, onward through life he (the blacksmith) goes," the inspector asked what toiling meant, and was answered correctly. Then he said to a white-faced half-timer, "What does rejoicing mean?" "Being jolly and glad," was the reply. "And why was the blacksmith rejoicing?" asked the inspector. "Because his wife was dead," said the half-timer. (The reader will remember that Longfellow's Village Black-smith is a widower.) The inspector laughed, and I with him, but there was a touch of sorrow in my laugh, for, knowing that half-timer's mother, I knew that the lad had answered feelingly, out of his experience and his father's.

Chapter IV

THE EFFECTS ON GIRLS

A few words now close the effects of the half-time system, especially on girls. I quote from

H

the pamphlet by Mr Waddington: "There are 22,000 little girls half-timers in Lancashire, 2461 in spinning mills, 9800 in weaving sheds, and the remaining 10,000 in mills containing spinning and weaving."[1] After describing the injury to health, he cites the figures giving the weight of factory children (see p. 103). The girls, being weaker, and more sensitive, naturally suffer more than the boys under the half-time system. It is a sad sight to see a batch of half-time girls, withered ere they have bloomed, and to think that these ghastly dwarfs are to be the mothers of the next generation.

Then, quoting from the Labour Commission, Mr Waddington says: "The general opinion of good mothers is that directly the child goes into the mill it is radically changed, and becomes coarse and vulgar. I maintain that mill life is not conducive to ideas of propriety, gentleness, and nobility in young children. Nay, I agree with a long-experienced factory inspector, who says: 'A large number of young female children, again, especially in the out-lying districts, are employed as doffers, an occupation which raises doubts in the inspector's mind as to whether it is, under the circumstances, calculated to promote morality.' Without scattering broadcast suggestions of immorality, there can be no doubt the

[1] According to the latest Statistical Abstract, published 1897 by the Government, there are now 25,432 girls under 13 years of age in cotton mills, etc., 11,788 in woollen and worsted factories, and 4754 in flax factories.

moral atmosphere of our factories is subversive
of that bending of the twig which ought to be
a very important phase of the work of the parent
and the teacher.   Entry in the mill is marked
by a growth of precociousness all too evident to
the teacher.   These little workers soon lose the
girlishness of their years, and soon the teacher
feels

> ' Ill habits gather by unseen degrees.' "

Mr Waddington further says : " The pleasant
fiction that half-time in the mill conduces to
educational progress receives its quietus at the
hands of ' My Lords ' of the Education Depart-
ment, who instruct their inspectors in the following terms :   ' In schools attended by half-time
children teachers have to contend with special
difficulties ; and in recommending the various
grants you may fairly accept a somewhat lower
standard of quality than in the case of other
schools, both as regards attainments and organi-
sation.'   Tested by whatever process, the half-
timer is found to be educationally handicapped.
But while in the subjects taken, the half-timer
is at a disadvantage, there is a still worse feature
connected with this mixing of work and education
—the curriculum has to be curtailed in the school
containing half-timers.   Generally, the half-timer
is educated alongside the whole-day scholar, and
in the North of England the curriculum of the
school is limited to meet the possibilities of the

half-timer, to the detriment of the whole-day scholar. Parents who refuse to sacrifice the physical, moral, and intellectual welfare of their offspring for the miserable pittance earned by these little workers, find the education ' cribb'd, cabin'd, and confined,' by the presence of these half-timers."

I still quote from Mr Waddington:

"The arguments in favour of the early employment of children have undergone very serious modifications during the last few years. Formerly the flexible joints of the infantile digit were necessary to the textile industries. But that argument is as hollow as the older one that little boys were necessary to go up chimneys, and reliance is now placed on the 'poor widow.' I do not suppose that Lancashire contains more 'poor widows' than any other county, but Lancashire employs 57 per cent. of the factory half-timers of the country. In Lancashire one-half the children over ten years of age work half-time, either in the mill or out of it. Are these all the children of poor widows? In the rest of England and Wales, after excluding Lancashire and Yorkshire, the proportion is only one out of every thirty-one. If half-time is the index of poverty, then the Lancashire artisan is in a dire state of destitution. There are badly paid artisans and poor widows in Lancashire, but these are not very largely the patrons of the half-time system. The comparatively well-paid spinners and weavers are the supporters of child labour; nay, they are the *employers of child labour*, because it is cheap labour, and they are paid 'by the piece.' Cease to make the spinner and the weaver the direct employer of the piecer and the tenter, and half-time would soon become a relic of 'the good old times.'" [1]

One thing more, and I have done with the half-timers, though much more, sad and startling, could be written. It is certain that many of the half-timers come from poor homes, and have to suffer for the carelessness, or idleness, or drunkenness of their parents, as well as—in the case of parents comfortably off—the greed of those responsible for their being. Mr Joseph Shufflebotham made what he calls "A Food Inquiry" concerning the children attending the Bolton Board Schools. He found many attending school without food, and here are the children's own reasons:—

"Kept in mill cleaning; no time to get dinner." (This was a half-timer.)

"Father out of work."

"Father in prison." [2]

Many children would sooner—at least, till the burden grows heavy on them—be at the mill than at school. Why?—Because of the horrible, forc-

---

[1] All these extracts are from "The Half-Time System as it affects Girls," by Richard Waddington; published by the Women's Emancipation Union.

[2] From "Something Attempted, Something Done."

ing, punishing "cram" of the present system of education.

And I do not dispute that you will find half-timers who like the factory. But why? Here is the reason. Because the mills are warmer, more comfortable than their homes.

From what homes these little wretches must come!

Well, is not this enough of an awful tale? These things are going on to-day—in England.

9. Weavers and Tacklers: a weaving shed in Swinton on Queen Victoria's Jubilee Day, 1897.

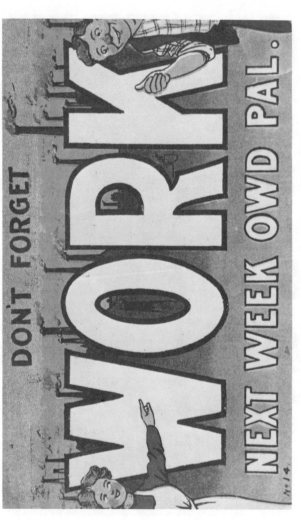

10. A reminder of the reality of working life at holiday time.

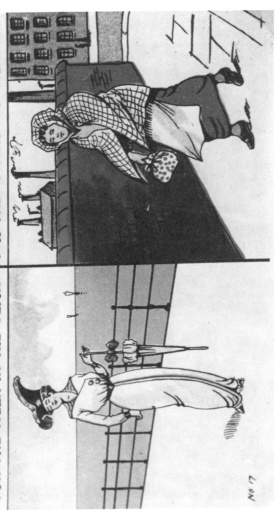

11. Work again next week.

19. Minder (far right) with side piecer, little piecers and others, Oldham c. 1900

13. Another day's work, the little piecer, Oldham c. 1900.

14. Prospect Mill's last days, Halliwell, Bolton 1984.

15. Bentinck Mill, Farnworth. Once a leader in the
West African Trade, semi-derelict, 1984.

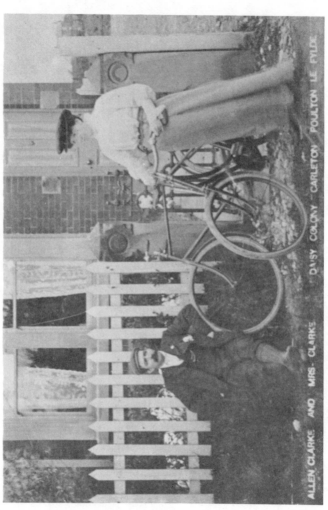

16. Allen Clarke and Eliza Clarke at Daisy Colony, Poulton-le-Fylde, 1905. The colony

INFANT MORTALITY IN FACTORY
TOWNS

AFTER the spectacle of the half-timers, this is the most heart-rending aspect of the factory system; though one cannot help thinking that the children who die before they are old enough to enter the mill are favoured by fate. For the babies are even less able to take care of themselves than the children.

After the facts stated previously concerning the debilitation of adults by the factory life, and especially the deteriorating effects on the mother, it will be obvious to readers of this article that children born in manufacturing towns begin life bitterly burdened with a hell of heredity from which, in most cases, there is no escape but death. A great percentage of infants in Lancashire manufacturing towns are still-born. This is no wonder; neither is it the least surprising, after seeing the conditions under which pregnant women work, that miscarriages in the early stages of gestation are very common. But for this fact the large families in the working population would be overwhelmingly large. Indeed, many of the factory women try to force miscarriages by means of pills, herbs, and all manner of tricks, such as standing on the table and jumping off, etc. Whether they do this for the benefit of the unborn child or themselves I cannot say ; but I think it is mostly out of consideration for themselves. Those women who work in the factory do not wish to have the trouble of a confinement, with consequent loss of wages and the addition of another mouth to fill. Scientific preventives of conception are not much in use among the factory operatives ; they resort to the clumsy expedients for abortion I have just mentioned. But this is a chapter not to be written here. I have merely mentioned it in passing to show that amongst the majority of factory mothers the birth of a child is not looked forward to with the longing love of pure maternity, but regarded as a disagreeable necessity, incident to sexual commerce. Indeed, there is little sweet and clean idea of fatherhood and motherhood amongst the factory workers. The babe is generally an unwelcome encumbrance, the result of fleshly accident, and, "to make the most of a bad job," as the Lancashire saying has it, is invested in some employment as soon as possible, in order to make some return towards the expense of his bringing-up, which " bringing-up " is mostly a scramble through picked bones, and not at all the food, education, and happy childhood which should be the unstinted heritage of every little child. I am glad to say, however, that there are many exceptions to this type of parent :

mothers and fathers who will sacrifice themselves
willingly for the benefit of their children; noble
women who will slave and starve themselves in
order to keep their children clothed and fed; who
will deprive themselves of necessities that their offspring may not be sent to the factory, but have
a better chance in life than their parents. And in
this connection I mention, with tearful sensation
and deepest reverence, my own mother and father.
I am proud to say that I know many similar
mothers. This last twenty years the sentiment
that parents have a holy duty towards their offspring has grown beautifully, and I pray that it
may spread far and rapidly; for these self-denying
and true parents are by no means the majority,
but only a small minority, often snubbed and
reviled by their neighbours for their brave en-
deavours to make the world brighter for their
children than it has been for them. Often in a
Lancashire town you'll hear some coarse woman
remark: "Ay, So-and-so's not sendin' their Jack
or Polly to t' factory; they're makin' 'em stuck-
up an' consated. But *my* childer will have to go to
t' spinnin' and weivin' whether they like it or not.
I had for t' do it, and so must they; what was
good enough for me's good enough for them
surelee!"

I have also known many cases where the
parents of young women weavers have made every
objection to their daughters getting married because they would rather keep them in the factory

for the sake of the wage. And in all these instances the parents have not been in hard need
of the money, and in most cases could have
done without it. But to feed their greed they
would keep their daughters in the mill as long
as possible, not caring that the girls were rendered
more unfit for motherhood by every additional
year spent in the weaving shed. Many Lancashire
mothers only love their children for what they can
get out of them.

Now to statistics on infant mortality in Lancashire : " The proportion of deaths of children under
one year of age to each 1000 registered births
was equal to 134 in the county (Lancashire), or 138
in the urban, and 109 in the rural districts." [1]

Here is a comparison of the infant mortality
in Lancashire manufacturing towns and rural
districts :—[2]

TOWNS.		RURAL.	
	Per 1000.		Per 1000.
Manchester	176	Birkdale	99
Salford	199	Grange (Morecambe	
Oldham	184	Bay)	41
Blackburn	171	Kirkham	84
Bolton	168	Levenshulme	86
Burnley	170	Morecambe	97
Preston	203	Much Woolton . . .	81

[1] Report of the Medical Officer of Health for Lancashire
for 1894.

[2] Report of the Medical Officer of Health for Lancashire
for 1894, and Annual Summary of Births and Deaths, issued
1896.

Towns.		Rural.	
Per 1000.		Per 1000.	
Wigan	189	Prestwich	83
Ashton	168	St Annes-on-the-Sea .	55
Rochdale	153	Turton	72
Stockport	189	Withington	90
Bury	178	Wiresdale and Wardle .	80

In all fairness, I must admit, however, that the infant death-rate is greater in some of the rural districts than in the towns. For instance, at Standish it is 209 per 1000, and at Blackpool, on the sea coast, 159 per 1000. But there are probably local causes (defective sanitation, sewage, etc.), to account for these high figures.

In the *Ashton Reporter* (November 23rd, 1895) I find the following letter :—[1]

"SIR,—If you will allow me a little space in your columns, I should like to allude to the note on the above subject which appeared in your issue of the 16th. Commenting on the discussion which took place in the Council Chamber on Monday, the 11th, and which showed the infantile death-rate to be 367 per 1000 for the quarter, or the enormous proportion of one-third of the births, your note says: 'One most naturally expects Ashton to be considerably above the average in this respect, owing to well-known

[1] I have not made any deliberate selection of papers for my purpose. I have just taken the first to hand while writing.

causes in connection with the employment of women. This can never be altered so long as the same conditions prevail.'

"This, sir, I claim to be one of the strongest arguments against the factory system. The workers are constantly reminded of how much they owe to the factory system, and what benefits it has brought them. I would ask, Where are the benefits? Doubtless some will point to the wages which the factory hands get, and to the jerry-made dresser or the cheap piano which are to be found in the houses of a few of the workers, or to the week's holiday at Blackpool, which can only be obtained by scraping and saving during the other 51 weeks of the year.

"But what of the smoky atmosphere, the dirty streets, the small ill-ventilated houses, huddled together under the high and frowning walls of the factory and workshop, where neither pure air nor sunlight can penetrate? What of the women and children who are forced to work long hours in the hot, grimy, and sickening atmosphere of the factory, in order to contribute to the father's insufficient wages, added to the anxiety as to wages and employment in the present, and an awful uncertainty, nay, a threatening outlook for the future? And what of the 'Slaughter of Innocents' which is the result of our women going to work in the factory, being thus forced to become alike mother, housekeeper, and bread-winner? Can we expect anything but weak women, unhealthy and puny children, and a high death-rate under such conditions?

"Councillor Mason says it is hardly fair to compare Ashton with country towns. And why? Because in the country we get pure air, pure water, clear atmosphere, fields, grass, and flowers, and these things never exist alongside the factory system.

"Councillors Kelsall and Andrew seem inclined to blame mothers for going to work and leaving their offspring to the care of an out-nurse. Surely no one would attempt to say that they go to the mill out of choice. As one who is constantly brought into contact with the lives of these people, I know that they are forced to go to work in order to keep their home together, and it is a deplorable fact that such conditions exist.

"Councillor Park speaks of the want of hygienic knowledge as responsible for much of the evil. Would Councillor Park tell us what is the use of further instructing mothers in hygiene, seeing that, as Councillor Cooke says, they have to go to the factory to work, and are thus deprived of the opportunity of practising what hygienic knowledge they have?

"In conclusion, I would suggest that if the Corporation would condemn all insanitary dwellings, and build comfortable dwellings (not barracks), which could be let at a reasonable rent, the difficulty in regard to slum property might easily be overcome. Thanking you in anticipation of insertion, I am, yours,

E. A."

That letter is, with one exception, a true statement of the case. The exception is, the assertion that no mothers go to the mill from choice. As I have elsewhere proved, many married women *do* go to the mill from choice, and especially till the birth of the second or third child.

In Manchester, in 1871, 9739 children were born alive; in the same year 2075 infants died. . . . The waste of infant life in Manchester, as compared with the rates for the whole of England and Wales, amounted to 535 children under one year of age. If you compare the Manchester mortality with the healthy districts' mortality, the waste amounted to 1070 lives.[1]

"The average age at death in all England is only 29. . . . In the large towns this is materially reduced, being only 21 years in Liverpool, and a little over that figure in Manchester. . . . Out of every 1,000,000 children born, about 260,000 die before their fifth year."[2]

In England the average age at death is 29

---

[1] Manchester Health Lectures: "Why Little Children Die," by H. H. Vernon, M.D. Published by John Heywood.

[2] Manchester Health Lectures: "Long Life, and the Causes that Prevent it," by Arthur Ransome, M.D., M.A. Published by John Heywood.

years, in France, 34 ; in Sweden, 31 ; in Surrey, 34.[1]

The Surrey child has therefore a chance of 13 years more life—and healthier life, too,—than the Manchester or Liverpool one.

The local statistics of the mortality of children under five years of age is too big a field to enter here, but they all prove that the manufacturing towns are far from being as healthy as the rural districts.[2]

Dr Brown (Bacup) says : "If the high mortality of our Lancashire manufacturing towns is to be permanently reduced, it can only be accomplished by married women making home-life and the claims of maternity their highest and most sacred duties. The 'feeding-bottle' has been a great factor in conducing to infantile mortality. It has made the way comparatively easy for a mother to leave the infant while she went to the mill. It should be looked upon as a most unnatural thing for a baby to have a feeding bottle. Every mother owes it as her highest duty to suckle her infant if possible. Thirty years ago, feeding-bottles were rarely seen. Now, they are everywhere in manufacturing towns. *No mother with an infant ought to be under the necessity of going to a mill,*

[1] Manchester Health Lectures : "Long Life, and the Causes that Prevent it," by Arthur Ransome, M.D., M.A. Published by John Heywood.

[2] See tables in Report of Medical Officer for Lancashire for 1894, or any year from 1870 to present time.

as it cannot be done without injury to the offspring."[1]

" Dr Hosegood (Swinton and Pendlebury, industrial district) sums up the causes of infant mortality as due to (1) improper feeding, (2) insufficient clothing with undue exposure, (3) inattention to personal cleanliness, (4) improvident habits combined very often *with gross and even criminal neglect.*"[2]

[1] Report of the Medical Officer of Health for Lancashire for 1894.

[2] Report of the Medical Officer of Health for Lancashire for 1894.

SECTION VIII

WAGES

CHAPTER I

MONEY WAGES

Now, what do the factory operatives get for their toil? What pay for this ruination of themselves and blighting of their children? For this loss of health and brain, this loss of fresh air and sweet recreation, this loss of limb and life, for all this cindery renunciation of the beautiful earth, what are they paid? Let us see.

In 1886, according to the General Report on the Wages of the Manual Labour Class (issued by the Board of Trade, October 1895), the average weekly wage of the adult male factory operative was 25s. 3d., of the adult female, 15s. 3d.; of boys, 9s. 4d.; and of girls, 6s. 10d.; the half-time lads getting 4s. 6d., and the girls, 2s. 3d.

The Board of Trade General Report on Wages, however, does not give a true idea of the real earnings of the factory workers. I fancy that the wages of piecers (adult, though really but apprentices) are averaged with those of the spinners (equal to journeymen). I give the correct wage figures for Oldham and Bolton, the two central towns of the cotton trade :—

OLDHAM

Average spinner's wage	.	. . .	35/-
,, big piecer's wage	.	. . .	17/-
,, little piecer's wage	.	. . .	11/-
,, cardroom hand's (male)	.	. .	26/-
,, cardroom hand's (female)		. .	18/-
,, half-timer's wage (male)	.	. .	5/-
,, half-timer's wage (female)		. .	2/6[1]

BOLTON

Average spinner's wage	.	. . .	38/-
,, big piecer's wage	.	. . .	14/-
,, little piecer's wage	.	. . .	10/-
,, cardroom hand's (male)	.	. .	24/-
,, cardroom hand's (female)		. .	14/-
,, weaver's wage (female)	.	. .	18/-
,, half-timer's wage (female)		. .	2/6
,, half-timer's wage (male)		. .	4/6[2]

If anything, the average wage is less now. It certainly is not more. In 1832 the adult male cotton operative's wage averaged 31s.; in the same year the adult female (weaver's) wage averaged 12s.[3] It seems the male wage has decreased,

[1] Supplied by Operative Spinners' Secretary, Oldham.
[2] Reckoned from Bolton Spinners' Annual Reports, and checked by personal inquiries amongst operatives.
[3] "The Cotton Trade in England and on the Continent" (Gævernitz, 1895).

while the female's has increased.   Here are some
further figures :—

Yarn Production per Operative.	Cost of Labour per lb.	Annual Wage of Operative.
1819 . . 968 lbs.	6.4d.	£26 13 0
1844 . . 2754 lbs.	2.3d.	28 12 0
1882 . . 5520 lbs.	1.9d.	44 4 0[1]

The worker thus turns out six times more stuff
than in 1819; but does he get six times more
wage?   Six times the 1819 wage makes £156.
But the worker only gets £44.   Where goes the
other £112?   The work is now done in considerably less hours, too.   In 1855 the factory
hours for adults were 82 per week; to-day they
are only 56.

The value of the wage depends, of course, upon
its purchasing power, and a shilling to-day will
purchase more than it would at the beginning of
the century.   But there is not much real difference;
for a shilling to-day will also purchase more labour
than it would in 1801—six times more than it
would in 1819; and if food is cheaper it is because
the labour is cheaper.   A man nowadays does six
times more for his shilling than in 1819, though
he does not get six times as much value for it—
perhaps not twice as much; and he always pays
dearly for the cheapness, gaining nothing really.
The lords of labour, whose conjuring tricks are

[1] "The Cotton Trade in England and on the Continent"
(Gævernitz, 1895).

the most exquisite delusions and bewildering prestidigitation, make it their business to see that the workman never gets anything but at his own expense. While they are making him believe that pennies are growing in his whiskers, they are dexterously abstracting his purse from his pocket; the money taken off the corn to cheapen his loaf is filched from him by subtle, roundabout ways. They pretend to give him gold sovereigns for a shilling; all he gets is a gilded sixpence. The manufacturers agitated against the corn laws because they hoped thereby to get cheaper labour. They were philanthropists when it paid. The Englishman can only get truly cheap bread by growing it himself; or, at least, by seeing that he is not cheated by the go-between party when the produce of his British labour is being exchanged for foreign corn.

Figures, though useful, rarely prove much; and seldom prove fully. Statistics can only show the truth in skeleton. For instance, what idea have you of the human body when you are told that there are over 200 bones in a man's osseous system, 68 lbs. of muscle, 10½ lbs. of skin, 28 lbs. of fat, 3 lbs. of brain, and 11 lbs. of abdominal viscera? Does that give you a picture of Shakespeare, or even a likeness of the meanest yokel? How, then, can any mere tables of figures give you a faithful and vivid depiction of the Lancashire factory system of to-day; of the ugly towns, the degenerate people, the suffering children, the hideous, monotonous toil, the dreary streets of barrack - like houses, the white faces going to and fro at their toil under the black skies? There is practically no more difference between one factory day and another day than between the 365 slips of calendar in the factory office, and these slips are all alike except that the figures differ daily for a month, from 1 to 31, then begin again; yet at a short distance they all look exactly the same.

<hr>

CHAPTER II

REAL WAGES—FOOD, HOUSING, ETC.

THE best way to get at the real value of the factory operatives' wage is to inquire what necessaries and comforts of life it brings them. We have seen the sort of town they get to live in. A brick box with a lid of smoke, which is very unhealthy. "Mr Estcourt, the city analyist, tells us that one ton out of every 100 tons burned in the factories of Manchester remains in the air as soot. This, in fog, is often productive of pain and a feeling of tightness in the chest; very oppressive indeed. All chest affections are made worse by it." This smoke is on all the houses, and even enters them, soiling furniture and clothes.[1] Let us look at the individual houses. They are

[1] Lecture on the Pollution of Air, by Henry Simpson, M.D. (published by John Heywood, Manchester).

mostly small four-roomed (two above and two below) cottages, rents varying from 3s. 6d. to 5s. 6d. They have no baths, as a rule. Each house is one of a long row, like a barracks, divided into so many equal portions. All cooking and cleaning are done in the living apartment; the washing is done in the room behind. On wet days the clothes are dried in the living room, to the discomfort of the husband when he come homes from the factory. The houses have generally scant backyard space; the jerry-builder wishes to squeeze as much property on the land as possible, and tries to cheat the building and sanitary authorities as much as he can.

Internally the cottages are cheaply furnished, though here and there some are set out luxuriously, mainly with intention to display and swagger over less fortunate neighbours. The more furniture a woman has in her house, the greater her social position. The women are proud when they can exhibit a parlour to Sunday visitors; it is shut up six days of the week, and is only kept for brag. Ostentatious superfluity, in the idea of the artisan's wife, is, as with those in higher grades of society, a sign of superiority.

Many of the houses are very meanly furnished. The piecer getting 14s. a week, has to be content with a table, a few chairs, and a bed. Often families of a dozen sleep in two rooms.

Gævernitz (whose book, translated by a factory master, is supposed to be a correct authority on the factory system) makes some very erroneous statements about the prosperity, housing, food, etc., of the Lancashire cotton operatives.

He is taken to visit various houses—selected by the employers or their secretaries, who naturally take him to the exceptional—even rare—specimens; spinners who are teetotalers, co-operators, and have a family of grown-up sons and daughters working. He says nothing of the time during which the families are being brought up; nothing of strikes, lock-outs, and other drawbacks; but makes Lancashire into a little heaven. He speaks of the mule spinner having a yearly trip to the seaside; a house with a garden in front (!); containing a piano (!); "and nowhere is the arm-chair missing for the head of the family." [1] He further describes the "well-nourished, well-dressed operatives," enjoying a holiday at Blackpool, all the males looking strong and healthy, the females fine and strapping; and states that there are no trade disputes, "masters and men working in thoroughly sweet accord."

A pretty picture, if it were only true. I have never seen it, though I have lived in a manufacturing town all my life, and not merely paid an exploring visit of a week or two's duration; neither have I seen the sturdy operatives at Blackpool, as Gævernitz describes, though I have resided there five years, and not got all my

[1] "The Cotton Trade in England and on the Continent" (pp. 173-200).

experience (as he did) on one brief day-excursion. My experience is, that there is one piano in about every hundred of the operatives' houses, and then only got when all the children are growing up and working, and generally on the hire system. Herr Gævernitz does not say whether the musical instruments he saw were paid for or not.

As regards the operatives' holidays at Blackpool, I have observed the factory visitors there for several years; and it is quite easy to single them out in the crowds, not because of their remarkably healthy looks, but the contrary. And I may ask, Is a few days' stifling, jostling holiday, in a town packed with excursionists any commensurate rest after fifty weeks' factory labour? When at the seaside, the factory folks work harder than at their daily toil, rushing to and fro in order to see everything in their brief sojourn, and they generally go home more weary and jaded than they are after a week's work. And most of the factory operatives never get to the seaside for more than one day a year; while a great many never get there at all, even on a day-trip.

Whatever be the wages of the factory operatives, they are mostly barely sufficient. They allow a breakfast of coffee or tea, bread, bacon, and eggs—when eggs are cheap; a dinner of potatoes and beef; an evening meal of tea, bread, and butter, cheap vegetables or fish, and a slight supper at moderate price; a few news-papers, cheap clothes, and sometimes a day or two at the seaside. The factory operatives have small chance of saving a competency for old age. Some few, by sore scraping and hard denial of all pleasures of life, manage to buy a house by the time they are ready for the grave; but most end their working period as poor as they began it. I never yet heard of any operative spinner retiring on the smallest fortune made by his factory work. Most spinners, when they became too old for the mill, used to start small shops or get a donkey and cart and vend greengroceries; but co-operative societies have closed those open-ings, and the worn-out spinner of to-day generally has to be kept by his grown-up children, or spin his last earthly set of days in the workhouse.

A friend of mine, whose employment sends him daily into working-class houses in several towns, sends me the following:—

"The facts which have struck me most forcibly are the following:—

1. The low wages of a large number of factory workers—married piecers earning 13s. per week. I have one family in my mind particularly. The husband gets the wage aforesaid. They have two children already, and a third just appeared. During the whole time of her pregnancy, the wife has almost up to the last moment been engaged day after day in taking in washing to supplement

the husband's earnings. She is now lying in bed with a baby at her side, and a tumour in her leg.

The most impressive fact, however, which I have come across is the extent of female labour and its terrible effects on the children and the home.

Female factory labour, whether single or married —but especially married, is the great curse of Lancashire. To take a pistol and shoot a man is moral compared with its effect. I will give you one or two examples.

No. 1. Married woman—works in factory. Up to recently she had one child. This child suffers terribly from fits, and probably will do all its life. Up to within a fortnight or three weeks of the birth of the second, the mother continued her work in the mill. The child is, of course, pining, ailing, sickly, and will probably never be fit for anything. The mother went back to work again two or three weeks after the child's birth. The child is left in charge of its grandmother, who is nearly worried to death by its perpetual wailing. The house is, of course, a pigstye. Yet they are very respectable people.

No. 2. Married woman—worked in the mill until her marriage—has had six children. Three of them died of convulsions. The last one of the three living is also terribly afflicted with convulsions, and the doctor says it may die in a fit any day.

And so I might go on to any length. There is hardly a house where the mother works or has worked in the factory but the terrible effects of factory life are seen in the physique of the children.

The effects on the home of married women working in the factory are simply awful. There is no home, and no home life. Pegged up in small jerry-built houses destitute of order or comfort. The mother sends or leaves her children to be nursed if young, and if not young, leaves them to look after themselves. At dinner-time she hurries home for a cup of tea and some bread and butter, and after this repast, hurries off back again to the mill. Ill or well, she has to go; children ill or well, she has to go; baby expected, she goes up to the last moment, and back again to the mill soon after it is born. Glorious life—this working in the mill, carrying an unborn baby and coming home to drudge at housework till bed-time.

Finding no home comforts, the natural thing follows. The husband, after his day's work is done and finding his wife helping to keep the home, goes off to the alehouse, and spends in many cases as much as his wife earns—and so the game goes merrily on.

No. 3. Another striking thing is the uncertainty of labour.

To almost every factory worker it happens that one fine morning work is slack, and one or two of the family have to stop at home till times mend. The earnings of the family are reduced, and they can't pay their grocer's bill. Sometimes the case is far worse than this. At Astley Bridge one mill has been stopped nineteen weeks, and has only just started again. During the whole of this time the employés are in a sort of semi-starvation, and running so far into debt for rent, etc., that it will take months or perhaps years to pay off all they owe. Long before they have paid all off the mill may stop again, and then debts will be a drag on them all their life.

Examples of all these I could give galore."

The factory operatives do not read much, and study little. As I have said before, their day's labour unfits them for any real mental work. They seek light amusement when their toil is done. They patronise the football matches in thousands. They want no lectures on science, ethics, culture ; they have no desire for art galleries ; they are so ignorant of Nature that they have little love for rural strolls ; all they crave is stirring excitement or full rest from their labours. And can we blame them ?

The Annual Report of the Bolton Public Free Library for 1894-95 gives us some interesting figures. During twelve months 7224 books were read or consulted by the cotton operatives ; out of these books 70 were theological works, 66 philosophical, 145 biographical, 196 historical, 93 on voyages and travels, 350 legal, political, or economical, 360 scientific, 115 poetical and dramatic, 2354 fiction, 561 magazines, and 2765 general literature ; total 7224. This does not mean a total of 7224 cotton operatives, but a total of 7224 books read by cotton operatives. One cotton operative may have had forty or fifty books in the course of the year. In Bolton there are at least 10,000 cotton operatives; so that if each read two library books once a year the total would be 20,000; as it is, it is only 7224; which shows, at least, that fully half of the cotton operatives are not frequenters of the public library. And it is quite probable that many of them who use the library merely went there because they were out of work and had nothing else to do.

The lending library figures are worse still. Only 80 male cotton operatives used the lending library in 1894-95. Eighty out of ten thousand! During the same year 62 clerks obtained cards for the lending library; that is nearly as many as cotton operatives. Yet in Bolton the cotton operatives must be at least forty to one compared with clerks. I should add that 43 female cotton operatives were borrowers from the lending library during the same period.

As with the mental, so with the spiritual. The cotton operatives are not, as a body, regular attenders at places of worship. They prefer "a good rest" on the Sunday; often lying in bed till nigh noon; for the seventh is the only day of the week on which they are not forced to rise before six o'clock in the morning. We, therefore, cannot censure them for having "a good rest" one day a week.

I give here the results of a religious census taken in Bolton in December 1896 (the figures will be found in the *Bolton Weekly Journal*, 25th January 1896):—

Population (1891 census) . . .	118,000
Estimated increase since 1891 . .	7000
	125,000
Number of young children, sick, working, absent, aged, infirm, etc., who could not be expected to attend a place of worship	45,000
Number who could attend . . .	80,000
Number of persons actually present at places of worship on Sunday evening, 22nd December 1895 . . .	14,000
Not present	66,000

The census was taken at the evening services. If it had been taken in the morning, the figures would have been still worse. Of course the 66,000 non-attenders at places of worship are not all factory operatives, and their families, though the bulk of them are, as Bolton is a factory town, and one-half of its men and women workers are employed in the cotton-mills and weaving-sheds.

Chapter III

TRADES UNIONISM, POLITICS, AND SOCIAL MOVEMENTS

THERE is one other thing to mention as an effect of the factory system : and that is trade unionism, which is the shield the workers were forced to make (under terrible difficulties) for protection against the employers. But, though trade unionism has been a fairly good shield, it is but a narrow one ; and, further, though the workers have often used it for purposes aggressive as well as defensive, it has never been anything but a shield, never a sword. And a shield, however strong it may be, is but a crude weapon to use in a fight. Indeed, we should smile if we read in any romance of a knight going to war with nothing but a shield as equipment. Mad old Don Quixote had more sense than that.

The operative cotton spinners (male) are exceptionally well organised in a trade union ; the female factory workers only moderately. The reason is, I suppose, that the young women are all looking forward to being married some day, and therefore do not think it worth while to join a union and pay for benefits they will probably never need.

I do not think there is one spinner in Bolton who does not belong to the union. The women's unions, weavers, and cardroom hands, are but poorly supported. And whatever the trades unions have gained has been hard fought for. Workmen were forbidden to combine, and punished for forming unions to raise wages in 1800. These laws were repealed in 1824, when modern trades unionism began.

The period of eighty years between then and now is a history of fearful struggle; of bitter opposition by the masters to the claims of the men. In 1800, journeymen of various trades were tried at the quarter-sessions, and imprisoned for combining to raise wages. There were bread riots; the people were in a state of semi-starvation. When trades unions first began to be formed (after the repeal of the Combination Laws) the "law declared the members outlaws; statutes were passed with the view of permanently stamping them out of existence." Thus, oppressed, punished, banned, trades unionism lived and struggled on, its course marked by strikes and lock-outs, till 1850-60, so on to 1871, when the law "put labour associations on an equality with all other associations," and no longer could "an officer of the union embezzle its funds with impunity," which had hitherto been the case, as till 1871 trades unions were not recognised as lawful institutions; and where cases of officers misappropriating the union funds came into court, the prisoners were acquitted, and "practically told they could rob the society without fear of legal consequences."[1]

[1] "Trades Unionism, Old and New," by George Howell, M.P.

The factory masters do not view the unions with much favour even to-day.

Gævernitz alludes to the "harmony" between masters and men in the cotton trade; but I must say that to me this harmony is not very conspicuous. Taking the *Factory Times* (for the week I write this chapter), I find a total of fourteen strikes, disputes, or threatenings in one week. There is such a record almost every week in the paper I have mentioned. This week, while revising this chapter (November 19th, 1897), there is a strike at Clitheroe in its eleventh week, two weaving disputes at Nelson, spinners' strike at Darwen, dispute at Colne, strike at Millgate (Facit), and strike at Burnley. Take almost any weekly issue of the *Factory Times* and you will find a similar tale. In addition to these there are lots of disputes that never get into print, but are settled privately by the operatives' secretaries and masters' secretaries.

A word with regard to politics and social movements amongst the factory operatives. The factory folks are, in the main, conservative, slow to change. They have no true idea of life. They believe that they are born to work; they do not see that work is but a means to live. They have no clear conception of our nation's system of work and trade. They cannot grasp the fact that our trade and commerce is the *effect* of labour, not the *cause* of it, as they think. They think that the masters build factories and

K

workshops, not to make a living for themselves by trading, but in order to find the people employment. They honestly believe that if there were no mills and workshops the poor people would all perish, because there would be no work for them, and consequently no wages. They cannot dissociate the products of labour from money-wages; they do not understand that money is principally nothing but a convenient medium for exchanging goods. They have no rational grasp of politics, or political economy, or the governing of the business of a nation; though, in their own little sphere, they are shrewd and quick-witted, and sensible enough. To make a simile from their own factory labour, they thoroughly understand how one machine—the one they tend—is worked, but they do not understand how a factory full of machines is worked collectively.

Politics, though, are much discussed by the more intelligent of the male factory operatives; but they seem unable to grasp the problem of government in its general sense, and always discuss particulars more than broad schemes. They are remarkably ignorant as to what politics or government really is. This peculiar mental state is undoubtedly caused by their work amongst machinery; as they know and understand little parts of the factory work, but have no notion of the whole mill as revolving round the engine-boilers, so they know and understand insigni-

ficant political details, but have no conception,
or only the haziest, of the plan and purport of
a nation's parliament. They actually do not
clearly know how their towns are governed.
There is also another reason for their befogged-
ness. They get all their knowledge from papers;
—it is most singular, by the way, what faith they
place in newspaper news;—and as the press is, in
the main, capitalistic, all important reports are
garbled and prepared ere they are printed, just
as when visitors are going through a mill, everything is arranged beforehand for them to see.[1]

In politics, the factory folks are chiefly conservative; though there have been, and are,
many exceptions amongst them; little groups
and bodies banded together for reform and
progress, and bold advancement. But most of
their combinative reforms have been defensive
—that is to say, selfish.

Trade unionism is merely collective selfishness;
the effort of a number of men to combine together
for their interests as a body. The same may be
said of the co-operative movements which started
amongst the factory operatives in Rochdale, Lancashire (1844). The aim of these founders of co-
operation was simply to benefit their own class—
the working folks; they did not care if they

[1] As a journalist I know how often reporters are requested
to suppress items of news (at Town Council Meetings, etc.)
that the manipulators of a town do not wish to be made
public.

injured the tradesmen, as they knew they must. Indeed, they fought for the interests of their own class, just as landowners or the aristocracy do.

The Chartist movement was different. It did not begin, as is often said and written, amongst the factory operatives, but amongst the hand-loom weavers whom the factory system was driving out of existence (1838). And the aims of the Chartist movement were wider and more generous than the aims of most of the movements inaugurated by factory folks. For the Chartists—the old hand-loom weavers—were men of some ideal; they loved nature, poetry, philosophy; and had visions of a whole world happy in the beauty of brotherhood. They were broad where the factory operatives are narrow, and had lovelier and loftier conceptions of the purpose of existence and the destiny and future of the human race.

The Friendly Societies and Burial Societies so common in Lancashire and the North of England have precisely the same objects as the Co-operative Movement and Trade Unionism, that is, the selfish protection of working-class and individual interests. It is pathetic to note the desire of the toilers for a "decent" funeral; they count a pauper's grave an eternal disgrace, and are so afraid of it, that one would think it meant to them exclusion from all hope of a heavenly hereafter. Indeed, the factory operatives are a great deal more anxious about their death than their life. They will stint them-

selves in life in order to have a satisfactory inter-
ment at its close.

I might state that the factory operatives are, as
a body, opposed to Socialism. They do not
join the Independent Labour Party either. Out
of 3000 spinners in Bolton, I don't think there
are a dozen belonging to the local Independent
Labour Party. I question if there are half-a-dozen.
Engels says "the factory operatives, and especially
those of the cotton districts, form the nucleus of
the labour movement."[1] That is true as regards
trades unionism, but no more. It might have
been true fifty years ago; but even on this point
I think Engels was mistaken. As I have stated
before, the Chartists were not factory operatives.
They came mainly from the hand-loom weavers,
whose home employment was being taken from
them by the power-looms. I do not think the
factory operatives have ever agitated for direct
representation in the Government of the country.
Though no class of the working community has
been so well legislated for as the factory operatives
yet they are the most opposed to State interference
to-day. They have always been content to think
that the masters whom they fought locally (with
trades unionism), would, when made into M.P.s,
suddenly be transformed from foes to friends, and
bless in London the constituents they cursed at
home as workmen. For one thing the factory

[1] "Condition of the Working-Classes in England in 1844,"
by Engels.

operatives have always been conspicuous — a stupid and stupendous faith, or perhaps credulity, would be the better word.

The Teetotal Movement, which also started in Lancashire, at Preston (in 1832), mainly holds forth the material advantages to be gained from a sober life, instead of advocating the righteousness and morality of temperance. Its lecturers and disciples are always pointing out the thrifty side of teetotalism ; what an advantage it gives a man over his intemperate fellows, and so forth. The result is that most teetotallers are very narrow and bigoted persons, who are teetotal simply from a scraping, saving point of view, and who, consequently, come not only to regard drinking, but even all innocent pleasures, as waste of time and money. I have found most teetotallers mean and grasping, devoid of all love of humanity, caring nothing for their fellow-men, so long as they were securely housed and fed themselves. And the teetotallers who have "got on," and become employers of labour, are generally the hardest and most skinflint of masters.

These things I write, not because I am against temperance, for I am a teetotaller myself, but because they are facts. The factory folks are teetotal, co-operative, and so forth, not from high motives, but from selfish motives, and it is the motive that makes a deal of difference. Indeed, it is the lack of the purest and highest ideals which is the curse of all the movements begun by the cotton operatives, as it is, perhaps, the curse of other movements working in other grades of society.

I am glad to say there is not quite as much drunkenness amongst factory operatives as there was twenty years ago, especially where the women are concerned. Bands of Hope and Temperance Societies have certainly done something. Drunkenness is now looked on as a disgrace, and not viewed with the good-humoured leniency or indifference it was twenty or thirty years ago.

Are the factory folks educated? Not in the real sense of the term—and not much at all in any sense. They get the ordinary elementary day-school education—now in board schools as well as denominational—but they forget most of it after they have left school for a few years. The grammar and geography entirely leave them, while they cannot forget history, because it is rarely taught them. And they have a false notion of education; they look on it only as a means to getting an easier living. With regard to their children, education is something the youngsters have to go through before they can go to work half-time or full-time, and nothing more. Indeed, as parents had to be punished by fines by an Act passed in 1844 to prevent them sending their children to work before the law permitted, so to-day most of them would not send their children to school if they were not forced. To-day the Lancashire operatives, almost to a man and woman, oppose the raising of the half-time age. And I can remember how angry parents used to be when the factory doctor refused to pass any sickly or small child for half-time; while the child itself was considered disgraced, and snubbed at home. "Education" in our elementary schools at the present day is not, as it ought to be, the drawing out and developing of a child's faculties, but the cramming into it of something for which it has no taste, and which it would generally be better without. In the matter of education, as in most other things, everything is for utility, or gain, and nothing for beauty or the pleasures of the mind. I have previously mentioned the "reading" of the working-folks in a factory town. But that was with reference to books. How with regard to papers?

Once more I take Bolton, because I know it best, and I only wish to write of what I know. In Bolton there are about eighty newsagents. Nearly seventy of them have joined together in a wholesale publishing society (on co-operative lines), getting their supply of papers direct from the publishers and distributing them amongst their members as demanded. Now this society sells more *Comic Cuts* than any other paper, and after *Comic Cuts* come *Tit-Bits*, *Answers*, and *Pearson's Weekly* — all scrappy periodicals, full of light reading matter that will not in any way make readers wiser or better, but simply muddle their minds with a ridiculous confusion. *Great*

Thoughts, *The Clarion*, and literary and reformative papers sell in the smallest quantities. On
the other hand, sporting papers are in the
greatest demand, and some of them at such
prices as a shilling daily. A great deal of
betting goes on in the factories and workshops
"Books" are made up, and "sweeps" arranged
amongst the men, who have never seen a race-
course or race-horse. There is also considerable
betting amongst the men's wives.

Papers containing serial stories also sell well;
especially those containing romantic love-tales,
wherein the poor working-class heroine, generally
a factory girl, marries a lord or rich man in the
last chapter. Cheap novelettes have a great sale
too.

In short, because of the monotony of their
working lives, the factory folks ignore all serious
thought or study in their leisure hours, and seek
all that is frothy and exciting in amusement and
literature.

Put into concise summary, the factory opera
tives' homes, food, clothing, education, amusements, morals, and religion, are all "manufactured
goods" mixed with a deal of shoddy. The stuffiness,
narrowness, frailness, and machine automatism of
the factory are part of their lives and souls. In
short, the factory folks have been reduced literally
from human heads to mere "hands."

In conclusion, I assert that while, on the whole,
the factory folks are better fed, better housed, and

better treated than they were fifty years ago, and that while a few of them get good wages, and live in parloured houses, owning a piano, maybe (after years of laborious saving), the majority live in small cottages, shabbily furnished, unblest by literature or music, pursuing an existence that is mainly from "hand to mouth," an existence that is pithily described in their own Lancashire phrase as "all bed an' work." The accounts which appear in London papers and magazines, of male cotton apprentices getting £3 per week, and female weavers getting £2 per week, should, by right, be relegated to the fiction portion of those publications. The cotton operatives, men and women, work hard, and work long, in hot stuffy air, midst eye-dazzling machinery, and ear-smiting thunder, liable to all sorts of accidents in the mill, liable, because of their occupation, to catch chest complaints when they leave the mill; getting few holidays and unable often to afford a holiday when the factory engine is stopped for this purpose; weakening and debilitating themselves physically, mentally, and often morally, and transmitting to their children their ruined constitutions and feeble frames,—all for a wage that would hardly keep my lady in gloves and bonnets, or my lord in cigars and wines.

But wages, either of individuals or nations, are not to be reckoned in pounds, shillings, and pence, but happiness and welfare. And in asking "Does the factory system pay?" the answer that it pays the country in gold, the master spinners and merchants in silver, and the operatives in copper, is an answer that proves nothing except that the country is rich in material goods, the masters wealthy in a base way, and the operatives not absolutely wanting, but getting, in the main, sufficient food to keep them alive for their work.

In the highest sense, in the truest sense, in the best sense, the factory system does not pay. The country whose work really pays it is the country whose inhabitants, man, woman, and child, are healthy and happy, who have leisure enough to improve their minds and bodies, to make the earth better and brighter for those who shall follow them, and who find the world not merely a place wherein to scramble for bread and butter, but a sphere wherein they may live in sweetness and cleanliness, enjoying its beauties and glories, studying its varied phenomena, trying to solve its mysteries, and enriching their being with the religions, and poetries, and philosophies, made out of this visible dust by invisible human spirit; in short, not a foul workshop, but a fair garden, wherein one may ponder heroically the problems of human existence and the purpose of this human life.

And all this—indeed, very little of it,—as we have seen in these articles, the factory system does not allow. Therefore it does not pay.

THE FUTURE

Chapter I

HINTS FOR REFORM

HAVING thus pointed out the evils of the factory system, perhaps it is only just that I should, at least, make some suggestions for remedying them. The chief evils are the effects on women and children (born and unborn). Reformative efforts should be, first of all, in the direction of prohibiting child work till the age of fourteen or fifteen, and secondly, in stopping married child-bearing women from working in the factories. Less hours should be worked, too; six hours a day are quite enough to spend in a cotton-mill or weaving-shed, and the work should not begin till 8 o'clock or 8.30. It is neither healthy nor wise to rush off to work without breakfast, at 6 o'clock in the morning, and toil two hours ere having a meal. Factory inspectors need to be more vigilant, too; at present the masters and managers of the mills always know beforehand when the inspector is likely to be about. Also, the workers should have more courage to complain when things are not right. Despite the "steaming" regulations, I have letters to show that the Act of Parliament is broken and evaded very frequently. The other day I had a letter from Heywood informing me of such a case; the weaving-shed is saturated with steam, but, when the inspector is about, the steam is turned off till he clears away.

Though I do not think, personally, that the factory system ever was good, and can hardly think that it ever will be good, yet I admit that it may be made very tolerable, perhaps almost pleasant, by improvement and amelioration in the directions I have indicated. It certainly is a burden and a weariness—and often a slavery—at the present day.

Yet, in spite of all its grim gloominess, there is a certain romance about the cotton manufacture. Seen from the outside on a dark winter's morning or black winter's evening, the great factories look like shining glass palaces, and make a pretty sight, one here, two there, another over yonder, and three or four in the distance; standing big above the little barracks-rows of cottages. Inside the mills, there is much of the marvel of invention which might inspire a poet to a verse or two; the wonderful machines, dreams of the human brain made strangely visible; quick, grand, terrific machines, working almost like giants superintended by dwarfs, more amazing in their strength and subtlety than any of the mighty genii of the "Arabian Nights." There is the magic of the spinning-mule, of the loom, and all the other machines, and one cannot help but admire these supreme contrivances, and could view them with delight if they were only rightly used—if they were the slaves of human beings, instead of human beings their slaves.

For there can be no question that most of this machinery was designed as a weapon against the worker, in case of strikes, and to reduce cost of labour, not to lessen the operative's toil and bless his life with leisure.

"It is, undoubtedly, correct that the self-act or spinning-mule, invented by Roberts in 1830, was designed as a weapon against the spinner, and first came into general use in consequence of strikes."[1]

I wish to repeat here, that I have written these articles as truthfully and fairly as possible. I know both sides of the story, and have tried to tell an honest tale throughout. I have no wish to injure or defame Lancashire, for I love my native county; I love its people, and would like to see them all happy evermore, amongst what moory hills and fair dales are yet unspoiled by the factory system. I love my kin-folk for the good that is yet in them, for the virtue that yet survives, sickly but not dead, like grass and flowers, struggling for life along a cindery railroad track— for the virtue that stirs many of them, in spite of the selfishness engendered by the system they

[1] "Philosophy of Manufacture," Ure, p. 367.

live in, to be so kind and charitable to their neighbours in time of affliction or distress, to be so willing, generally, to make sacrifice for the good of others; and there is yet strong amongst them one saving quality from which I hope much —the sense of humour. In every factory and workshop there are a few bright cheery spirits who keep their mates alive with joke and fun, full of a humour that, though often cruelly chained and lashed by privation, yet smiles and will not die, but frolics even in grime and steam, and makes the world sweet and kin with human mirth.

Chapter II

DECLINE OF THE LANCASHIRE COTTON TRADE

WHETHER we will or not, we shall be forced to do something by-and-by. We cannot keep the world's cotton trade for ever. Already there are ominous signs that it is gradually leaving us; other nations are rapidly competing with us. Many men competent to judge are of opinion that the Lancashire cotton trade—so far as applies to export—is doomed. For the last three or four years all the reports of the cotton trade have been very depressing; mills stopping, people out of work, factory operatives unable to get employment. The cause of this, naturally, is the decline of our exports in cotton goods. In the golden period of the cotton trade, 1871-1881, our exports were much more than now. In 1881, we exported cotton goods to the value of £58,404,212; in 1893 the value of cotton goods exports had fallen to £47,281,114. Since then there have been slight risings and fallings; but it is clear that the main tendency is decline.

On the other hand, the cotton goods imported to England from abroad are valued at £1,040,748 (in 1896). In 1883 they were only half that, £520,897. Put along with these figures our exports of textile machinery, and we shall understand why our cotton trade is declining. In 1882 we sent to foreign countries textile machinery to the value of £7,053,480 (or rather less, because this includes all other machinery except agricultural and locomotives). But in 1889, 1890, and 1891 we exported yearly over ten million pounds worth of machinery, and nearly as much in 1892. And we are still exporting it at the rate of six million pounds worth per annum.[1] This is bound to tell a tale, and is telling it now to all who can read with understanding.

For many years now Lancashire men have been hard at it building mills abroad, and teaching the foreigners how to spin and weave. To-day the great machine works of Lancashire are almost entirely engaged in fitting up mills abroad. Very few new mills have been erected in the shire of the Red Rose these last five years. Once on a time (1775) India protested at import

---

[1] Figures from "Statistical Abstract."

duty being set on her cotton goods sent to England;[1] to-day, in the inevitable irony of things, the grievance is reversed, and Lancashire is complaining wofully of the duty put on her cotton goods sent to India.[2]

From 1870-1881 the cotton operatives flourished on fat wages. They were the lords of labour: the manual aristocrats. The great mills were bright with business; the men were merry with money; their labour was not all a burden, but part a recreation; and the manufacturing towns were painted with the happy hues of prosperity. The foreigner had not yet begun to build many factories; England had not put into the hands of other nations those knives of competition with which they might cut her throat, selling for a little present gain, weapons that in the future would be used against her to her hurt.

The spinners, or "minders," were the working aristocracy of Lancashire; they strutted in the shoes of importance, and talked with the voice of superiority. They breathed the upper air; joiners, bricklayers, moulders, colliers, and others were mere rabble whose noses sniffed the dust of the ground. Cotton was power and glory; timber, iron, coal, and clay were vulgar inferiority.

"No spinner with any self-respect in his stomach would drink beer in the taproom with a common

[1] Gævernitz's "Cotton Trade in England and on the Continent."

[2] See any newspaper for November 1895.

L

labourer; he must have his ale clad in shining glass, not paltry pot, and enjoy it in the company of his own class, or at least with engineers and other artisans of the elevated grade, who had the time o' day and night told to them by gold watches with conspicuous chains to match. Amongst the blue-blooded and wealthy upper circles, there could not be any sterner divisions of caste than those separating one section of working-folk from another at this time. The cause of this is easily found. Trade was flourishing, and there is nothing makes people more independent than well-doing. Good fortune, in a state where all kinds of fortune from surfeiting to starving may exist side by side, sets people apart from one another; misfortune draws them together. Wealth dwells in little isolated groups; poverty huddles in crowds. A communion of sorrow is a surer bond than a communion of joy; this is one of the strange facts of human nature. Later on, when trade declined and woe came upon labour, all sorts of workers, high and low, were eager to join together to do something remedial. But in these days, when all went well, when no sullen population of unemployed menaced the security of those lucky in toil, when no harassment of to-day foreboded evil for the morrow, when no wages were being brought down to bare subsistence point, nor reductions being resisted with all the suffering and misery of strikes and lock-outs; when no empty bellies set empty heads a-thinking and organising labour agitations to demand justice for the workers: in these days the high noon showed no shadow of the coming night, the workers never considered the benefits of brotherhood (except, perhaps, in the narrowness of separate unions, each haughtily going its own way), but ate up the juicy present with a relish, and did not think that the future might consist of only the picked bones."

There are many signs that the Lancashire cotton trade is doomed. The unemployed are greatly on the increase amongst cotton operatives, especially in Oldham district.[1] Young men brought up as "piecers" (*i.e.* a sort of apprentice) cannot get "wheels" (or become journeymen spinners), and vast numbers of them go to overcrowd the "labouring" and kindred occupations. Recruiting sergeants, knowing of this state of things, have even taken to advertising in the cotton operatives' newspaper.[2] Formerly piecers, if competent, could usually get "wheels" soon after the age of twenty; now, unless they have a relative or friend in the manager or overseer, their chances are scant indeed. Further, there is almost daily rumour in the air of the masters' intention to reduce wages, on the plea that they are now running their concerns at a loss. While one does not expect

[1] According to the *Northern Daily Telegraph* for November 8th, 1895, there were even then 5000 mill hands out of employment in Oldham and within a radius of twelve miles.

[2] *Factory Times*, 1895-96.

absolute truthfulness from a master cotton-spinner, when speaking of the pecuniary side of his business with a view to lowering wages, all these hints have an ominous meaning.

I now proceed to quote the opinions of authorities on the state of the cotton trade. These opinions I gathered together in 1895-6 (when I was compiling this book), but they are just as true now—nay, are more accentuated and more significant than when first uttered.

Mr Wm. Mullin, secretary to the Lancashire Card and Blowing Room Associations, said: "The Lancashire cotton trade was in a deplorable condition."[1] . . . Then, in an article in the *Factory Times* for November 22nd, 1895, entitled, "Our Trade: a serious Question for Consideration," Mr Mawdsley, the secretary of the Amalgamated Associations of Cotton Spinners, says: "Much as we deplore the fact, there can be no question that the countries of Eastern Asia are more and more preparing themselves for an onslaught on the cotton trade. We are not going to moralise on the fact that the great bulk of the cotton machinery at present being made is for export, though that is a matter which might well be considered. . . . Our export trade is, and must remain, the backbone of our business, and it is consequently abroad that we shall have to look for any relief worth having." After stating his opinion that the cotton trade can be improved

[1] *Northern Daily Telegraph*, November 15th, 1895.

by opening out markets in Asia, South America, and the colonies, Mr Mawdsley goes on : "But although we are sincerely anxious to see the best side of the cotton industry, we are bound to admit that, looking at matters as they actually stand, . . . we see no probability of the trade being able to absorb an increase of population in the future. The trade will certainly increase, but not more rapidly than improvements in machines, which will allow the same number of hands to meet the increase."

So, even when brightened by Mr Mawdsley's ostrich optimism, the position remains a dark and dismal one. When we have opened out the new markets ('tis a great *when* that, and what of the meantime ?), Mr Mawdsley can hold out no hope of the cotton trade being "able to absorb an increase of population." Will it even absorb the thousands of cotton operatives already out of employment ? And how is Mr Mawdsley going to stop population increasing ? By trade unionism, eh ?

The foreign markets from which Mr Mawdsley expects so much are already being opened up by others. The Egyptian Cotton Company is building at Cairo ; and "many persons are watching the inception of this enterprise with eagerness, as to other ventures to follow."[1] While spindles in Lancashire have only increased by 50,000 in three years, those in other parts of the world have

[1] *Factory Times*, November 22nd, 1895.

increased over three and a half millions in the same time. Of this increase, over a million is in India, China, and Japan.[1] In India the increase in spindles and looms during the last fifteen years has been 270 per cent. ; increase of hands, 300 per cent. ; increase of cotton consumed, 425 per cent. ; and while in Lancashire mills were standing idle and thousands of operatives out of work, thirteen new mills were in course of erection in India.[2]

Where's the hope for the Lancashire cotton trade? Very few, if any, new mills are being built in Lancashire. I only know of one near Bolton—a limited company—and in order to have a chance of getting work at this place candidates for employment have to take up at least one £10 share (1896). So keen is the competition amongst the unemployed that it seems the workers must now also find capital before they can have work. Speaking at a banquet in connection with the opening of the new Cotton Exchange Buildings at Liverpool, January 4th, 1896, Mr C. W. Macara said he hoped "every man, woman, and child in Lancashire who earned their bread by the cotton industry would take to heart the weighty words uttered by Mr R. S. Platt, the great machinist (Oldham), who said that the Lancashire machine shops were now so largely employed on foreign orders that the cotton

---

[1] *Factory Times*, November 8th, 1895.

[2] Report of speech by Mr George Whiteley, M.P., in *Northern Daily Telegraph*, November 17th, 1895.

operatives of Lancashire had better realise in
time that a reduced wage-list was preferable to
none at all."

Of course, the cotton operatives, knowing well
their humble place in the commercial scheme
of this country, must not say a word against the
English capitalists who are making fortunes by
putting up foreign mills to the ruin of home
trade. What they must do is gracefully prepare
for less wages.

"Speaking at a meeting called to hear a scheme
for dealing with the unemployed," says the
Yorkshire *Factory Times* (December 27, 1895),
"Mr Councillor H. Whiteley, J.P., made a speech
which should be studied by every worker in the
textile industry. He said he happened to be
engaged in a business (textile) which was bound
to leave the country largely within the next twenty
years. . . . What with the coming expansion of
manufactures in the Far East . . . there seems
to be a future of anxiety ahead of the textile
operatives, which demands more careful thought
than nine out of ten are prepared to give. We
do not despair of the end, even if the worst comes
to pass, the restless energy of a busy race will ever
find some outlet for its forces. . . . To make
the change with as little pressure as possible,
and to be prepared for any sudden emergency,
it behoves every thoughtful operative to watch
the trend of events, to read and educate himself
to take an intelligent part *in the closing struggles*

of a gigantic trade, and to take that part manfully and unselfishly."[1]

I now add a few facts of more recent date, though there is hardly any need to say anything further to prove that the Lancashire cotton trade is dying. The *Pall Mall Gazette* of December 30th, 1897, says: "There is concern at the growing development of cotton spinning in China, and particularly at Shanghai, where there are now nine mills, and six more at Hankow, Wuchang, and other cities in the interior." In the evening papers for January 24th, 1898, I find particulars of the development of the cotton trade in Mexico. In 1895 we exported 51,479,100 yards of cotton goods to Mexico; in 1897 only 39,266,400 yards. In 1889 there were only 5394 women and 2537 men employed in the Japanese cotton trade; in 1895 there were over 30,000 women and 10,000 men.[2]

The cotton trade is also developing on the Continent, and America is becoming a formidable rival. In the United States there are already 221,586 cotton operatives, almost half as many as in England. We have also to face American labour-saving inventions, particularly the Northrop loom.[3]

The factory masters, in their greed, are going the way to cut off their own trade, eventually, by equipping other countries to compete against us.

---

[1] Italics mine.—Author.
[2] *Northern Daily Telegraph*, August 19th, 1896.
[3] *Factory Times*, December 27, 1895.

The great machine-making firms of Lancashire are almost entirely engaged on foreign orders—sending out spinning-mules, looms, and engines, and fitting up cotton factories in all parts of the globe : really creating that "foreign competition" which they urge as a reason for reducing wages at home.

The value of machinery exported during October was £1½ millions, an increase of £318,000 ; the increase since beginning of 1895 being £731,000.[1]

The effect of this is seen at home.

"Cotton operatives are complaining bitterly of the difficulties they are experiencing in finding employment, and they assert it is not alone in their own trade, but in every other kind of work their applications for a job meet with the response, 'We are not in want of any hands.' As for going round to the mills and workshops to find employment, the people say it is worse than trying to find a needle in a haystack."[2]

Trade Union returns sadly corroborate the preceding statements. In two years the 20,279 members of the Amalgamated Operative Spinners' Association have decreased to 18,341—a decrease of 1938—nearly 1000 a year—"or what would be required to work 77 of our modern mills."[3]

If the capturing of foreign markets is all we may depend upon, it is clear that the cotton trade is surely doomed.

[1] Board of Trade Returns for October 1895.
[2] *Factory Times*, November 8th, 1895.
[3] *Factory Times*, November 8th, 1895.

I wrote to Mr Alfred Hill, secretary of the Operative Spinners', Bolton, asking his opinion as to the future of the cotton trade, and he replied that he had not had time to formulate any opinion on the subject, . . . but while he was "very hopeful for the future of the Bolton trade, indeed, more hopeful than for the Oldham trade," he had not the time to thoroughly enter into the matter.

I am sorry to have to shatter Mr Hill's bright hope; but I suppose he knows that cotton mills are being put up at Cairo, which is right on the spot for the Egyptian cotton that keeps Bolton going.[1]

And George Harwood, M.P. for Bolton, and himself a cotton spinner, said, not long ago, in a public speech, that in his opinion the future Manchester would be Alexandria; which is a well-founded opinion. Alexandria is a geographical centre of the business world; it lies equal between East and West, and is of splendid and easy access for Asia, Europe, and Africa; cotton is grown in the country; and the moist atmosphere over the delta of the Nile is extremely favourable for spinning purposes. How will Lancashire secure those future "ifs," Mr Mawdsley, when Alexandria seizes the developing cotton trade of Asia and Africa?

No; we cannot hope to play much longer the buckswashing game of shooting Africans and other unoffending folks and stealing their land.

[1] See page 165.

One could think better of our rulers if they told the truth. Under pretence of spreading Christianity and civilisation, England has burned and blasted her way into foreign lands—merely to make a market for her goods, and to keep her slaves at home well employed. We support the sending of missionaries and Bibles to cover our naked grab. Our masters say it is all done to make trade and keep our workers at home busy. The truth is that they care not a jot for civilisation, nor Christianity, nor the glory of England, nor their work-people, nor anything but the enriching of themselves. They oppress one set of people at home in order that they may oppress another set of folks abroad; and English working-man and foreign barbarian (?) are alike whipped down.

Thus have our governors and rulers (whom every Sabbath we beseech—and not without cause—God to endow with wisdom!) sacked the whole world, and had all the spoil, except the fractions they give to the Crown for finding them soldiers and sailors to push and defend their interests, heaped round them, and when the crumbs and remnants of the feast have fallen amongst the working-classes they have said, as Dives would have said to Lazarus, "Look what we have done for you, and yet you are thankless!" What they have done they have done because they could not help it; they have only let the workers take the droppings, the spillings, which must needs tumble out of their basket of abundance in the carrying.

I would not for the world (being a conscientious scribe) deny that latterly (I mean this last thirty years) the working-classes have got crumbs where they formerly starved; wherefore they had begun to think their position prosperous, their condition congratulative; but now, alas! the master's basket is no longer brimming over, but failing, and even the crumbs but fall sparsely now.

More facts and figures could be adduced, but those so far given are sufficient to show that the Lancashire cotton trade is doomed. Not that it will die quickly: the actual end may be years in coming; the process will be more of a slow shrinkage than a galloping consumption. But the fatal symptoms are already unmistakable, and the end, speedy or delayed, is sure. Pauperism is on the increase in Lancashire, though in England, as a whole, there is a decrease.[1] And with our cotton trade will fall the English factory system, whose effects I have depicted in these articles. And, when we consider all the horrible sufferings the factory system has caused in the past,—the torture of children, the pain of women,—not alone in factories, but in coal-mines, which would not have been as necessary but for the factory system,—the sweating of men—and the burden that it is to-day, is this coming downfall to be regretted?

It is never well to prophesy doom or foretell bad news, but surely the northern factory folk, the folk

---

[1] *Manchester Evening Chronicle*, May 6th, 1898, commenting on statistics just issued by Government.

who have laughed and cried over my humble
everyday stories, who have cut out of their papers
and pasted in scrap-books my factory songs and
ballads, and know them as well as I do, who have
roared with hilarity over my humorous dialect
sketches, and have by heart all the comical doings
and sayings of my "Bill Spriggs," and whose
children have been delighted for years with the
"Corner" I specially conduct, and the tales I write
for them: surely these folks will never hate me—
one of themselves, a factory lad, son of factory
father and mother, brother to brothers and sisters
in the factory to-day, a faithful comrade and
their best well-wisher—for showing them the truth,
and praying for their salvation.

Chapter III

VISION AND HOPE

We have now made a thorough examination of
the factory system of to-day, and its effects. We
have seen the towns in which it is carried on;
we have seen the operatives, their homes, their
little smoky lives. We have seen the children,
and the cruel effects of the factory system on
them; we have had a clear glimpse of the whole
hideous business in all its ugly aspects, past,
present, and future. That there is some sweetness in all this bitterness, some light even in all
this darkness, I do not deny. Human nature

is generally optimistic under the most depressing conditions; soot, grime, squalor, poverty, torture, cannot utterly annihilate love and human affections. " Hope springs eternal," and men and women, even in the midst of the most crushing surroundings, especially if they have been familiar with them since birth, and know of nought better, set to making the best of the case, and can snatch, in moments of exalted forgetfulness, bits of joy and mirth from the skeleton hands of the boniest misery. Adaptability ameliorates all things; would even alleviate in time the pains of that tremendous place of eternal punishment, which many factory operatives, who cannot in the least be suspected of humour in this connection, grimly and religiously believe in to-day. Yet, in spite of these few trifling testimonies, which I willingly concede, for the other side of the question, I think I have conclusively demonstrated that the factory system of to-day is an evil thing.

I would like to see Lancashire a cluster of small villages and towns, each fixed solid on its own agricultural base, doing its own spinning and weaving; with its theatre, gymnasium, schools, libraries, baths, and all things necessary for body and soul. Supposing the energy, time, and talent that have been given to manufacture and manufacturing inventions had been given to agriculture and agricultural inventions, would not there have been as wonderful results in food-production as there have been in cotton goods production? Not that I think this would make a perfect state and millennium of happiness, nor even result in absolutely smooth comradeship; for human nature, however high it may grow towards heaven, is always rooted in earth. But even this ideal realised, would make wonderful and joyful difference; and under such conditions much of the jealousy, the spite, ill-feelings and passions, fostered by the present competitive system would certainly be gradually and marvellously modified. Good health has a deal to do with temper; healthy people are always tolerant. There are men and women who, even under the best form of communism, would have to be constantly watched and guided like children; men and women who are really nothing more than whiskered and child-bearing babies; the men, shiftless, with a knack of going wrong, unable to think or act for themselves: women incompetent to expend a wage economically, to keep a house tastefully, lacking tact and prudence, and who would always be in difficulty, no matter what income they had: but this sort are to be pitied and helped; they are probably victims of heredity. Two generations living in good healthy surroundings would make an amazing difference for the better in the third generation. And filthy centuries of folly cannot be mended in five minutes.

I have wondered whether Lancashire could not grow its own cotton—in hot-houses that would not be hotter than the mills, and certainly not a fraction as unhealthy and uncomfortable. If so, this would make a great employment for a considerable part of the population, and, with simple care, no injurious effects would result from the workers having such a change of temperature when quitting the hot-houses for their homes. Tropical fruits, too, could be cultivated at the same time in these hot-houses, which could thus be made into delightful gardens, as well as useful growing grounds, for the inhabitants to stroll in during the natural winter of their own climate.

Mr R. Cunliffe, Bolton, an authority on cotton-growing, and teacher of the Co-operative Society's technical class in cotton-spinning, etc., writes to me : " Cotton can be grown in hot-houses—I have grown some myself and have a few pods,—but not to such an extent as to be of use for manufacturing purposes."

But why not in sufficient quantities for manufacturing purposes ? Modern science could soon overcome the few difficulties, which are practically none at all. If foreign countries are beginning to do their own manufacturing, why shouldn't we begin to do our own growing ?

And thus we stand. While England has been growing great in certain directions, while inventions have changed the thought of the world, and overcome the opposition of Nature, while our literature has been sunned and starred by Dickens, Thackeray, Eliot, Tennyson, Browning, Carlyle, Whitman, and a hundred lesser luminaries, the condition of the working-classes has only moderately improved, and the factory system yet curses the land. With the exception of one or two writers—Mrs Browning for one—our literary lords and ladies have ignored the factory system as much as the landlords and worklords, and left the people to droop without word of protest or song of sympathy. None but the workers' own writers and poets have sung for them; and these have generally been neglected and forsaken by the class whose woes they sweetly tried to force on the notice of an indifferent world.

I do not wish to rouse class hatred and opposition. I wish to unite rather than dissever. Though the masters in the past, as a body, have been cruel to the men, a more humane and considerate spirit is astir to-day; and though there are yet unfair and tyrannical masters, there are also unfair and unreasonable men. This trouble should make a bond of union, not a gap of strife. A little love does more than the greatest measures. Indeed, it is from the sympathetic and intellectual ministers of the Gospel, doctors, journalists, and brain-workers of all kinds, aided by the more intelligent and advanced of the manual labour classes, that I expect any and all signs of hope for the future. The working-classes have always been slow to help themselves; the inspirational impulse and initial movement in any upward and beneficial

M

direction have generally come from outsiders. It will have to be so to-day. From the good men of all sorts the help will have to come—from employers who wish to do the right thing and just; from preachers who follow Christ; from writers who write for truth's sake, not Mammon's; from the lovers of humanity and self-sacrificers in all grades; from the noble army of apostles, and often martyrs, male and female, separate in hut or hall, in poverty or riches, but all one in the desire to do their duty to their fellow-women and men — not forgetting the children.